The Interactive Whiteboard Revolution

Teaching with IWBs

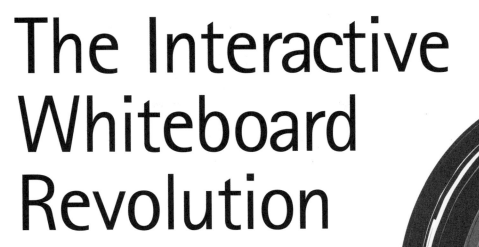

D0974045

Chris Betcher and Mal Lee

ACER Press

Special thanks to Linda for her love and support during the writing of this book. Her suggestions, encouragement and endless patience with the many late nights played a major role in helping me see this through to the end. C.B.

First published 2009
by ACER Press, an imprint of
Australian Council *for* Educational Research Ltd
19 Prospect Hill Road, Camberwell
Victoria, 3124, Australia

www.acerpress.com.au
sales@acer.edu.au

Edited by Ronél Redman
Cover design by Andrew Ritchie
Text design based on design by mightyworld
Typeset by Polar Design Pty Ltd
Printed in Australia by BPA Print Group

National Library of Australia Cataloguing-in-Publication data:
Author: Betcher, Chris.
Title: The interactive whiteboard revolution : teaching with IWBs
            / Chris Betcher, Mal Lee.
ISBN: 9780864318176 (pbk.)
Notes: Bibliography.
Subjects: Interactive whiteboards.
            Teaching--Aids and devices.
            Educational technology.
Other Authors/Contributors:
            Lee, Malcolm, 1944-
Dewey Number:
            371.33

FOREWORD

In early 1995, I was teaching at Blackburn College in the UK. I was invited to a local factory to view a prototype interactive whiteboard, or IWB. As a classroom teacher I had always been interested in how computer technology could enhance student learning. At that time I was learning desktop publishing on a DOS-based PC and also had two BBC computers at the back of my classroom. The realisation that the IWB could allow a computer screen to be displayed to an entire class—and the potential this offered—was something that amazed me. Later that year, I persuaded my head of department to purchase one. Our college became Promethean's very first customer, and to the best of my knowledge I became the first UK teacher to use a Promethean board in the classroom. Shortly afterwards, I joined Promethean to become their first full-time employee and, as it turned out, IWB 'evangelist'.

Little did I realise that this was to be the start of a worldwide revolution in the classroom, starting in the UK via the City Technology Colleges and spreading outwards like a tsunami over the next decade. With the continuous cost-down behaviour of projection technology, growth accelerated proportionately. Interestingly, the major growth and development area for IWBs has been in the K–12 education sector, and this has not been with hand-me-down technology from the commercial sector or higher education.

What has excited and stimulated me more than anything has been the way 'ordinary' classroom teachers have adopted the IWB, adapted their lessons and teaching styles and innovated using the IWB software. Not only has this kick-started or re-ignited their passion and enthusiasm for teaching, but it has also been very timely in engaging and motivating our 'digital native' learning population. It delights me that the most commonly stated reason why teachers adopt these boards so readily is that after seeing a board in action teachers immediately see the potential it offers for their day-to-day work. This is exactly what got me involved at the outset.

I always wanted to write this book, but have never made the time for it. This book should have been titled 'Everything You Need to Know about Teaching with Interactive Whiteboards', and whether you are an old hand or a complete 'newbie' you will extract gems from every chapter. I trust you will enjoy every page as much as I have enjoyed my IWB journey, which has taken me from my classroom in the northwest of England to the whole world—so far!

Peter Lambert
Interactive whiteboard pioneer
Director of Product Marketing, Promethean, Georgia, USA

CONTENTS

FIGURES

ACKNOWLEDGEMENTS

Writing this book has been the result of many conversations with leading educators about what works well in their schools and classrooms. While we have attempted to synthesise all the current theory and research about IWBs, we have also tried to view that research in the light of how it applies every day in real classrooms. The authors would like to acknowledge and thank the many wonderful educators who have so willingly contributed their thoughts, viewpoints, ideas and experiences. Their contributions are greatly appreciated.

Lesleigh Altmann (Aus.) Brette Lockyer (Aus.) Kyle Stevens (USA)
Tom Barrett (UK) Jess McCulloch (Aus.) Sue Tapp (Aus.)
Tobias Cooper (Aus.) Katie Morrow (USA) Paula White (USA)
Simon Evans (NZ) Cathy Nelson (USA)
Louise Goold (Aus.) Amanda Signal (NZ)

We would also like to thank the following people who at various stages read and critiqued the original draft. Their comments and feedback have been invaluable in helping to shape this book into an authentic document that reflects real-world teaching experiences with IWBs.

Anne Baird
Tom Barrett
Tobias Cooper
Faraday Pang
Susan Sedro

SOURCE ACKNOWLEDGEMENTS

Figure 7.1 — Reprinted with permission from The Sanborn Map Company, Inc. © The Sanborn Map Company, Inc. (2009).

Figure 7.2 — Reprinted with permission from Google SketchUp.

Figure 7.3 — Reprinted with permission from Markus Hohenwarter, GeoGebra.

Figure 7.4 — Reprinted with permission from Gapminder <www.gapminder.org>.

Figures 8.1, 8.2, 8.3, 8.4, 8.5 — Reprinted with permission from Lesleigh Altmann, Kempsey, Australia.

Figure 8.6 — Poem reproduced with permission from Amaru Entertainment /Estate of Tupac Shakur

Figure 8.7 — Screenshot reprinted with permission from BBC <http://www.bbc.co.uk/schools/magickey/adventures/patch_game.shtml>. Characters from the Oxford Reading Tree/Magic Key created by Alex Brychta, copyright © Oxford University Press are used by permission of Oxford University Press <http://www.oup.com/oxed/primary/treetops/index.html>.

Figure 8.8 — Reprinted with permission from Primary Games <www.primarygames.co.uk>.

Figure 8.10 — Image: Flickr user nasmac <http://flickr.com/photos/40775750@N00/1348038445/>.

Figures 8.11, 8.12, 8.13, 8.14, 8.15 — Reprinted with permission from Tobias Cooper, Presbyterian Ladies College, Sydney.

Figure 9.1 — Reprinted with permission from Tom Barrett, United Kingdom.

Figure 9.2 — Reprinted with permission from Jess McCulloch, Victoria, Australia and Wikispaces.

Figure 9.3 — Reprinted with permission from Susan Tapp, Australia.

Figure 9.4 — Reprinted with permission from Ben Hazzard, Canada.

Figure 9.5 — Reprinted with permission from Darren Kuropatwa, Dean Shareski, Wesley Fryer, Sheryl Nussbaum-Beach.

Thank you to the parents, students and teachers who allowed their photographs to be used in this book.

Every effort has been made to acknowledge and contact copyright owners. However, should any infringement have occurred, ACER tenders its apology and invites copyright owners to contact ACER.

CHAPTER 1

THE REVOLUTION

The first revolutionary teaching tool—the humble blackboard—found its way into classrooms back in 1801 and had a profound impact on the nature of teaching over the next 200 years. The blackboard became synonymous with the traditional classroom and, along with shiny red apples, is still seen as a stereotypical symbol of education. The interactive whiteboard—or IWB—has the potential to be the second revolutionary teaching tool. Just as the blackboard was seen as a key part of nineteenth- and twentieth-century classrooms, the IWB has the capability to become synonymous with the new digital classrooms of the twenty-first century. Despite its relative newness, the IWB exhibits the same capacity to fundamentally change—and indeed revolutionise—the nature of teaching.

In the same way that the old-style blackboards were a technology that could be used in traditional schools every day by all teachers, interactive whiteboards are already displaying their facility to be used in this 'every-day-by-every-teacher' way in our emerging digital schools. Because of their capacity to become an embedded part of a modern classroom, the IWB may just serve to be the catalyst that finally moves schools away from the traditional paper-based model towards a more integrated digital mode of operation. The traditional paper-based school has existed in more or less the same form literally for centuries, but we are starting to see the beginnings of a shift as schools all over the world start to look for ways to maximise the potential of digital learning and take advantage of the evolving and exciting educational opportunities this digital world brings with it.

However, we need to remind ourselves that this is still just the start of the revolution. The real challenges for teachers at this point in the development of digital classrooms are to see the great potential that lies ahead, to master the tools and the mindset to begin claiming that potential, and to collaborate with their colleagues and students to effectively use these new tools for teaching in a digital world. The IWB has all the characteristics for being a potent tool in this educational shift.

THE IWB CONTINUUM

As any new technology arrives, it will inevitably be used initially to continue doing many of the same things that the old technology could do, gradually moving on to reinvent some of the old things in new ways. If we observe most teachers as they begin to work with an IWB, we will probably see them making this shift by converting many of their old paper-based tasks into an equivalent IWB-based task. This is normal behaviour and to be expected as any new technology is adopted, explored and eventually tamed. But we need to remind ourselves that this approach is really just 'old wine in new bottles'. Ultimately, if the true potential of these new tools is to be fully realised, there must come a point where teachers start to think in completely new ways; not just to begin using the technology to do things that are merely a digital version of the old, but rather to create entirely new things that were not possible with the old technologies.

IWBs can let educators do more than just continue with the old ways. As interactive technologies become an accepted part of today's digital classrooms, new and previously unimagined ways are being found to use technology to enhance the teaching and learning process.

In seeking to realise this revolutionising potential, it is important to understand a little of the:

- context within which teachers of the twenty-first century will be working
- shortcomings of the earlier teaching tools
- factors that set this technology apart from the many other instructional technologies that promised to 'revolutionise' teaching in the twentieth century, and
- effective uses of this new tool in the classroom.

SETTING THE STAGE FOR A DIGITAL CLASSROOM

Right now, in classrooms around the world, what classroom tools do teachers use most on a day-to-day basis? According to a 2007 study, the most commonly used instructional technologies (other than the teacher's voice, of course) are still the pen, paper and teaching board (Lee & Winzenried, 2009). This is an important understanding because it highlights a key premise about why interactive whiteboards are different to many of the 'revolutionary' classroom technologies of the past. As a concept, the teaching board is a well-understood tool used by teachers to help perform the job they do in their classrooms every day. This is a great starting point. It acknowledges that while there are many technologies teachers may not be comfortable with, the humble teaching board is already a well-understood part of the way a classroom works. Of course, for many classrooms, those teaching boards are still the old-style blackboards (or green or white ones), but the underlying idea is that a shift to interactive technology as a better, more capable teaching board is essentially a case of rethinking an existing concept that most teachers are already familiar with rather than forcing them into a whole new way of working.

This chapter opened with the statement that interactive whiteboards have the potential to be the second revolutionary teaching tool, and teachers may be thinking: 'But what about the personal computer? Didn't that revolutionise the way we teach?' The PC certainly has had—and will no doubt continue to have—a huge impact on classrooms all over the world, but in most cases it is still more of a learning tool for students than a teaching tool for teachers. There is no argument that the personal computer has been revolutionary in almost every way imaginable and its impact over the last 25 years has been enormous, but when we look at its impact on the actual act of teaching, it is still relatively minimal. In a world where so many industries and professions have been completely reshaped and redefined by the advent of the personal computer, one could argue that the act of teaching (as opposed to the act of learning) has been largely immune to such technological advances.

There are plenty of reasons that account for this. The small screen size does not easily facilitate teaching in a group setting, and most non-IWB classrooms do not have a mounted projector ready for use. The PC is far more engaging when one gets to interact with it on a personal level, so it often fails to be an effective teaching tool in classrooms where the teachers are the only ones with a computer in front of them. The opportunities for connecting students with highly relevant and engaging digital content are enormous, but without some way of sharing those resources on a whole-class basis, the potential of the PC for the purpose of teaching with these resources is fairly limited.

As a tool for connecting teaching to learning in a digital world, the interactive whiteboard appears to be the missing link.

MORE THAN JUST WORKSHEETS

While many teachers use a computer to assist them in their lesson preparation, personal organisation and communication, most of this relates to managing their own individual productivity rather than any systematic way of changing their teaching practice. Although there certainly are some teachers who do make regular use of computers and other digital tools in their teaching, they are still in the minority. The truth is that most schools that claim to be reliant on personal computers only have 20–30 per cent of teachers using those computers with students in any sort of consistent, integrated, meaningful way.

Many students in our schools would be lucky to use computers in class for two hours per week. And these are just the schools where students are able to get regular, or semi-regular, access to computers for learning in an individual situation. Trotting the students off to the computer lab once or twice a week to 'do computers' is hardly an integrated use of technology across the curriculum. However, the prevailing situation is that most teachers simply do not have enough access to the digital tools in their classrooms to allow them to work with their students in a predominantly digital way.

One of the great challenges for schools today is figuring out how to get *all* their staff—and not just some of them—to embrace the use of digital technologies as a normal part of classroom teaching. It is still somewhat of a rarity. There is, however, strong evidence to suggest that it can be achieved—swiftly and relatively inexpensively—by the wise introduction of interactive whiteboards throughout the school (Lee & Winzenried, 2009). Figures from the UK indicate that there were only 5 per cent of teachers nationally using IWBs in 2002; however, by 2007 that figure had skyrocketed to 64 per cent (Becta, 2007). It is this sort of immersive growth that will enable IWB technology to become a standard part of a teacher's daily practice.

There are a number of factors that make IWB technology different to any classroom technology that preceded it. To see IWBs in their proper context, we need to bear in mind the points discussed as follows.

1   **IWBs are really the first electronic instructional technology designed primarily for use by teachers.**

All the other electronic technologies, be they film, radio, television or personal computers, were first designed for the general consumer or office markets and then eventually adapted for use in education. For almost all of these products, schools were very much a secondary market. In contrast, the first SMART Board was sold to teachers at a university in 1991, and the first Activboard was sold to a university in the mid 1990s. There are now dozens of other players in this space, all pitching their products specifically at the education market. Because IWB technology was conceived specifically with education in mind, most vendors are displaying considerable commitment and responsiveness to the needs of this market.

Also, although we keep referring to 'interactive whiteboards', it would be a mistake to restrict our thinking to just the board itself. It is worth remembering that there are also a rapidly evolving set of accessories designed to extend the concept of classroom interactivity beyond the board … wireless slates and tablets, interactive voting devices, interactive text response systems and so on. These devices add further depth to the possibilities afforded by the whole 'IWB' concept, and in fact hint at the real power behind this technology—not so much the board, but the interactivity.

2   **IWBs are the first and, as yet, only digital instructional technology that all the teachers in a school are able to use in their everyday teaching.**

While grand claims have been made by both governments and technology corporations about the amount of various technologies that may exist within a school, the research undertaken by Lee and Winzenried (2009) in *The Use of Instructional Technology in Schools* reveals that in 2007 those schools who had deployed interactive whiteboards throughout the school had 100 per cent of their teachers using digital resources in their everyday teaching.

Of course, this is not to say every school that deploys them will automatically get 100 per cent success in integrating technology just because of the existence of the IWBs. Simply putting IWBs in classrooms is no guarantee of success. However, it does suggest that, of the schools who did achieve 100 per cent integration, the implementation of IWBs was consistently a factor. To put it simply, a decision to deploy IWBs throughout a school substantially increases the chances of getting teachers to shift to a more digital mode of working.

Ultimately, success requires far more than just putting IWB hardware into classrooms, but it seems to be a critical part of getting there. After that comes a whole lot of professional development and training as well as rethinking about how these twenty-first century classrooms should work, but in many instances where classrooms are succeeding to do this, the IWB has played a pivotal role in the shift.

In reviewing the vast investment made in digital technology in UK schools since the mid 1990s, Becta, the British education authority, made this historic observation:

> This sharp rise in the use of ICT resources in the curriculum has been driven to a large extent by the adoption of interactive whiteboards (IWBs) and related technologies. Interactive whiteboards are a popular technology, in heavy demand by schools and practitioners. They offer transparent benefits to learning and teaching. That is, it is easy for institutions and teachers to recognise how IWBs enrich and enhance learning and teaching—something which may not always be so immediately transparent to practitioners in the case of other technologies.

> (Becta, 2007, p. 66)

Although computers have been around in schools for over 25 years, there are still many teachers who resist their use in any sort of regular, embedded way. Research suggests that IWBs seem to be acting as an effective 'gateway' for many teachers to start exploring the further use of digital technologies in their classrooms.

3   IWBs can be readily, securely and inexpensively installed in every classroom for immediate teacher and student use.

One solution to getting technology into the hands of learners is the implementation of a one-to-one program, such as where every student is issued with a notebook computer. While getting computing devices into the hands of all students is a worthy goal, the financial and logistical challenges in doing so have made this an unrealistic option for many schools at this point in time, and raises a whole set of new problems that most schools are just not ready to even start thinking about. Some schools have attempted to provide a notebook computer for every student; however, the widespread success of these initiatives has so far been restricted to a relatively small number of privileged schools. This may change in the future, but for the moment having available a computing device for every student in every classroom in every school remains a challenge.

On the other hand, interactive whiteboards are showing their ability to be used successfully every day, with all age levels, in all areas of the curriculum, with all types of school systems. IWBs are pervasive in ways that notebook computers have not yet managed to be. They are proving themselves to be an effective digital instructional technology with the flexibility to reach students on a consistent basis within all types of learning organisations, and within the constraints and givens of everyday schooling.

4   IWBs can accommodate all teaching styles and can be used to support whole-class, small-group and personalised teaching.

Interactive whiteboards can be just as readily used by the senior teacher preparing students for a public exam, the special education teacher working with students with learning disabilities, a distance education teacher working with remotely located students, a teacher using a highly differentiated discovery-based approach, or the kindergarten teacher working with five-year-olds. The boards can be used in a variety of ways—from a simple board for writing notes and drawing diagrams, right through to a fully integrated, multimedia-enabled, large-screen digital convergence facility.

However, not everyone is so positive about the technology. One of the main arguments used to dismiss the impact of the IWB in modern classrooms is that it heralds a return to the 'sage on the stage' mentality of teaching; one where the teacher assumes the position at the front of the class and the students passively consume the knowledge being dispensed. This form of teacher-centric classroom would quite rightfully be seen as a return to the bad old days of schooling, and if used in this manner IWBs are really nothing more than an expensive electronic way of 'chalk and talk' teaching.

However, anyone who has been in a classroom where this technology is used well, where the teacher is a competent and creative user of the IWB, where effective digital resources are being used to spark the learning, and extras such as interactive voting devices are being used to engage students in thinking more deeply, will quickly realise that there is nothing passive about these sorts of lessons. As always, good teaching is good teaching, and technology—if used correctly—can enhance teaching in all sorts of engaging ways. Any classroom technology can be used poorly if a teacher is not skilled and proficient in its use.

Contrary to the views of some sceptics, IWBs can be used in ways that dramatically enhance good teaching. When viewed simply as a piece of hardware, the IWB does not make the learning experience any better or any worse. What makes the difference is the teacher who understands how to tap into the potential of this new technology to create engaging, interesting, interactive lessons that capture the attention and imagination of the students in pedagogically sound, creative ways.

5   IWBs facilitate the integration and ready use of all other digital technologies—hardware and software, and give additional educative power to those other technologies.

At their simplest level, interactive whiteboards are primarily large-screen digital convergence facilities. Their educative potential resides in this facility to be used as the centrepiece of a digital teaching hub with an ever-evolving suite of digital tools to take teaching into the digital era.

While they may at first seem like just a fancy version of the traditional teaching board, IWBs can be used in fully interactive ways that are able to bring together digital resources like text, images, audio, video, 'dragable' objects and, of course, a seemingly infinite collection of resources from the web. Concepts can be explored, data can be manipulated, scenarios can be tinkered with … when all one's resources are available in digital form, the possibilities are almost endless.

So, those teachers who still think of IWBs as nothing more than expensive projector screens are probably not using them correctly!

With this ability to act as a convergence facility for a huge multitude of digital resources, IWBs are becoming somewhat of a Trojan horse for getting technology into classrooms where it may not otherwise have been able to penetrate. Evidence suggests that when armed with an IWB and training in the proper ways to use it, good teachers with a sound understanding of effective pedagogical principles are able to embrace a wider range of digital technologies more quickly and find more creative ways to engage their students with those resources.

6   IWB teaching is receiving immense and growing support from the 'IWB industry' globally.

The support provided to schools and teachers by the manufacturers of IWBs is particularly strong. With their focus on the competitive education market, it is in the interest of the IWB hardware and software providers to listen carefully to teachers, respond to their needs and continue to provide them with the best possible tools, teaching resources and online communities.

In contrast, computer manufacturers do not have the same vested interest. The education market is relatively small compared with the corporate market, and this is reflected in the limited educationally relevant software provided with most PCs. Despite what most computer manufacturers may try to tell you, their focus is clearly on the office, not the classroom.

Contrast this to the teaching software provided by the major IWB providers. Most of it is of high quality, focused on the classroom and constantly evolving. It is generally included in the price of the boards and the upgrades are usually free. Most major vendors will license their software in such a way that teachers can install it on both their work and home computers, all at no extra charge—and some may even encourage its use for students. Of course, it is in the manufacturers' vested interests to get as many teachers and students as possible using their software because this translates into many people using their hardware. But regardless of whatever commercial motives they may have, educators are the ultimate beneficiary of this competitive marketplace.

Sitting alongside the interactive multimedia teaching software provided with the leading IWB hardware is a rapidly growing body of commercial teaching software available for use with the boards. A visit to the likes of the UK-based Curriculum Online website (http://www.curriculumonline.gov.uk) will provide insight into the huge range of generic and subject-specific interactive multimedia teaching resources on the market. In Australia, a huge library of educational resources is available through The Learning Federation (www.thelearningfederation.edu.au), a federally funded project to build a massive repository of digital Learning Objects. These Learning Objects, or LOs, are freely available, developed by teachers for teachers, and work beautifully in an IWB environment. Similar projects exist in other parts of the world, such as the Co-operative Learning Object Exchange (http//cloe.on.ca) being put together by the University of Waterloo in Ontario, Canada, or the Wisconsin Online Resource Center (www.wisc-online.com/) who have developed a freely available library of nearly 2500 LOs. These are just a few of many such organisations busily developing Learning Objects that work exceptionally well on an IWB.

Then there are the thousands of teachers, schools, education authorities, broadcasters, museums, universities and foundations, all building resources for their own use and freely sharing them in extensive online communities. Websites such as Promethean Planet, SMART's Educator Resources and Easiteach, to name just a few, provide places where global communities of IWB users can freely and willingly share ideas, insights and files with each other. The value of these online communities should not be overlooked and perhaps ought to be the biggest reassurance of all that an investment into interactive technology is a good decision.

Of course, these new digital resources are in addition to the existing resources teachers have always used, be they software, videos, DVD, free-to-air and satellite TV and, yes, even print. The versatile nature of the IWB means that teachers can use their existing resources just as easily as they are able to explore the myriad of new ones. Then of course there is the whole world of possibilities that opens up when teachers begin to explore the read/write offerings of Web 2.0 …

And this is just the beginning.

DIGITAL CONVERGENCE

Suffice to say that at this stage in history the potential of digital resources to enrich teaching and improve student learning is immense. But for those of us still coming to grips with the technology revolution taking place in our classrooms, what does it actually mean to 'be digital'? What exactly is 'digital convergence' and why does it matter? What does it mean when we say that IWBs can act as a 'digital hub' in our classrooms?

To understand what it means to be digital we need to remember that prior to the introduction of the personal computer, different media existed in different physical forms. Text was something that existed on paper, photographs were taken on plastic film covered in silver powder, moving pictures were stored on long rolls of celluloid, video existed as magnetic impulses stored on tape, and sound had to be captured on some form of magnetic-tape medium such as cassettes. The problem with trying to integrate any or all of these media types together was that their differing forms made it difficult for them to 'play together' nicely. Teachers who had to put together a slide show the old-fashioned way with 35-mm slides would have realised quickly that there was no easy way to synchronise the music to the pictures except by some trial and error. Likewise, prior to computers, if a teacher wanted to write some text and then illustrate that text with a picture, it was a complex matter to stick the picture into the text. Any teacher who is older than the personal computer will probably remember that 'cut and paste' quite literally meant cut and paste—with scissors and glue!

All that changed when the computer appeared on the scene. Because computers store all media types in a common format—a series of zeros and ones known as binary—the task of combining different media types suddenly became a fairly trivial problem. To a computer, all these media types look exactly the same. In the early days of personal computers it was really only feasible to manipulate text and simple pictures, but as the power of PCs has grown over the last decades we are now in a situation where our machines have the grunt to easily manipulate and mix almost any digital media—text, audio, images, video, animation.

Then in the mid 1990s, Tim Berners-Lee invented the World Wide Web and we gained the ability to easily move these digital bundles of zeros and ones around the planet in mere seconds. It is now hard to find any area of human endeavour that has not been affected by the Internet in deeply profound ways, and we are rapidly moving towards a world where the entire sum of human experience will be available online somewhere. Finally, because of the nature of digital resources, they can be stored, viewed, manipulated and presented on a wide range of hardware devices, from mobile phones to interactive whiteboards. Suddenly, information is everywhere, and with the right device we can put it to work for us in ways that were unimaginable even five years ago.

Simply stated, the equation goes like this:

easy manipulation of a wide variety of media types	+	effortless ability to move these media types around globally	+	ability to interact with these media types on a wide range of devices	=	digital convergence

And it is rapidly changing the world.

For many of us who have been teaching for a while, these are scary notions. But to most of our students this is the only world they have ever known. Children entering our schools now do not know what it is like to not be digital, and while many of the things that seem like black magic to those of us who have been around for a while, to our students they are just an expected part of the way the world works.

THE POTENTIAL OF THE DIGITAL HUB

So what does all this mean for schools still thinking about how to embrace digital technology and, in particular, interactive whiteboards?

The reason why IWBs are often described as a 'digital hub' is that they are able to pull all of these digital experiences together into one place in the classroom. The logical place to do this is on a large screen where all students can see and interact with the media, and where teachers can engage students in discussion and exploration. IWBs are ideal for combining this digital content in an integrated manner so that, instead of a classroom where text is written on a blackboard, pictures are shown with an overhead projector, video is watched on a TV, the Internet is explored in the computer lab, and so on, all of these digital assets are now able to be pulled together and explored by teacher and student together in a manner that simply makes more sense—whether that means easily showing snippets of video relevant to the topic being taught, getting students to record their voices in a podcast and presenting it to their peers, exploring the pages of the web together, or for any number of other uses that simply were not possible before all these resources went digital.

If we all accept the premise that this new digital world is worth making an integral part of our classrooms, then IWBs make enormous sense. Otherwise, what are the options for embedding this digital content into our classrooms without IWBs? Trotting off to the computer lab once a week? That is hardly an effective strategy for making the digital world an integrated part of our classrooms. Give every student a personal computing device? A nice idea, but for most schools it is still a long way off for a number of valid reasons including cost, equity, logistics and more. This is why the IWB makes so much sense. As a large-screen, digital-convergence device, accessible to all students, affordable for all schools and easy to adapt to regular classroom use, this is a technology whose time is right.

CHAPTER 2

IT'S NOT ABOUT
THE HARDWARE

We need to be perfectly clear—this is not about the hardware.

When just starting out on the journey to bring IWB technology into the school, those in charge are probably grappling with a ton of questions about choosing the right whiteboards, locating them in the right rooms and making sure they are properly installed. It is likely that they are poring over a number of quotes from various suppliers trying to work out who will give the best deal. They might be coming up with a professional development plan for teaching the teachers how all the 'cool' features of the interactive software work, or they might even be planning a presentation for the next parents' meeting, ready to dazzle them all with the 'whiz-bang' things this new technology will bring to the classrooms of their children.

And while all of these things may be important steps in the process, if we don't take our thinking to the next level, we risk wasting a great deal of time, money and human capital. *Because it truly is NOT about the hardware.*

The ultimate success of interactive whiteboards in the school will be dependent on the same factor that defines the success of almost every other initiative that takes place within a school: the quality of the teaching and learning. Without quality teaching and learning based around a solid understanding of sound pedagogical principles, IWBs will be just another piece of hardware in the classroom. Unless teachers understand how to leverage interactive technology to create better learning experiences for their students, then we are wasting our time. Like every other technology in a school, IWBs should be used to stimulate student thinking, encourage deeper and more robust discussions, provoke thoughtful ideas and make abstract concepts easier to grasp.

Good teachers understand that while IWBs may be helpful and interesting, at the heart of it all is good-quality teaching.

Experience and research (Lee & Winzenried, 2006, 2009) have shown that the value brought to the classroom by an IWB can either be completely transformational or barely worth the trouble, depending on a few critical factors. Implemented wisely, IWBs can raise the learning across the whole school and take even the best schools to a higher and more exciting plane. Implemented poorly, there will be very little noticeable change, which will include wasting of money and having unhappy, frustrated teachers.

A TECHNOLOGY DESIGNED FOR EVERY CLASSROOM

To get the most from the school's interactive whiteboards, the ultimate goal is to have all the teachers and students in the school using them as a normal part of quality teaching and learning. Implementation will be successful only when the boards are used seamlessly and easily by all staff—as much a part of the classroom as pens and paper.

So the secret to making this all work is—first and foremost—to make sure that all the teachers understand the principles of good-quality teaching, built around a student-centred, constructivist model of learning. Second is the provision of enough resources and training to enable all staff to embrace the powerful possibilities this new technology can bring to them, and help them learn all the necessary new skills to effectively embed IWBs into their daily practice. The use of interactive technologies should be made an accepted and expected part of the way every teacher in the school delivers good-quality learning experiences to their students.

It all sounds simple enough; however, in practice it is not quite so easy to achieve. For a start, it would be unusual for all the teachers in the school to have the same understanding of pedagogy, the same level of enthusiasm for this new technology, the same willingness to learn and the same eagerness to adapt the way they teach.

With regard to technology, teachers tend to fall into one of three broad categories. In most schools there will usually be the early adopters who get excited about jumping on board with any new technology. These are the easy people to work with; they see the possibilities of interactive technology right away, quickly pick up the basic skills and are prepared to fumble their way through the rest, quite comfortable with the notion that they do not have to know everything about it just to get started. These people will willingly be the trailblazers, the pioneers, the ones for whom an IWB offers yet another exciting way to work with their students.

Then there will probably be a larger group who are interested but a little wary. They see the things the IWB can do and will admit that some of these things do look pretty 'cool'. They can see how the technology could probably be used to do interesting things in their classes, but they are not quite sure that they could learn how to use them, how they can fit in yet one more thing on top of their already busy curriculum and how it could actually improve grades and test results. These are the teachers who are not too difficult to persuade as to the value of the technology, although it may take a little time for them to get up to speed. But once they do make that breakthrough, many of them will wonder how they ever taught without an IWB.

In all likelihood, there will also be a third group of teachers. This group is not so excited about these IWB gadgets and instead of seeing amazing possibilities, they see a whole lot of obstacles to be faced. Some may be dubious about their worth, some may be quite negative and some may even be downright hostile to the idea. They cite all the reasons why IWBs will not work, ranging from logistical issues, timetable issues, resourcing issues or equity issues. Some will openly say that they think IWBs are a waste of time, that they could buy a whole lot of textbooks for the same amount of money, and that they will never use the technology. Perhaps they simply cannot see the educational value of using this technology, or they fear that using them will waste valuable teaching time. It may be a concern about how comfortable they will feel having to use them regularly, or they may be worried about that intimidating feeling of having to use technology in front of students who they think know more about computer gadgets than they do themselves. It may even be based on past bad experiences with the reliability and dependability of computers generally.

The temptation is to work with the first group, and certainly for a while this may be the best way to build momentum and get started. But remember what we said earlier: the ultimate goal is to have ALL the teachers and students using the boards as a normal part of the teaching and learning. And this is one of the reasons why it is not about the hardware. You can do all the research, install the best equipment and have the latest software, but unless you can make this school-wide cultural shift in the way the teachers think about how learning takes place in the school, there is a long, tough battle ahead.

TAKING A WHOLE-STAFF APPROACH

So as teachers begin to think about how to get an interactive whiteboard for their classroom—particularly if they have seen them used elsewhere and cannot wait to start using one themselves—they need to remember that there is a lot more to making them a success in the school than their own personal enthusiasm. It is very easy for one or two keen teachers to get an IWB and become total advocates for their use, but there is so much more to be gained by working collaboratively with the whole staff and developing a whole-school approach to their use. A few early adopter teachers can only do so much; it is when they win over the entire staff that they will see the real potential being realised.

Having said all that, any moves to bring IWBs into the school will in all likelihood begin with one eager and enthusiastic early adopter. Nearly all technological innovation will begin with these people, but the trick is not to let it remain with them. As the school embarks upon its IWB implementation, it must have a well-defined plan to get the use of IWBs out to as many staff as possible, as quickly as possible.

IT TAKES LEADERSHIP

The other major factor for success is strong leadership. It certainly helps to have a visionary principal demonstrating committed leadership to an IWB program as this is usually the best way to bring some of the less enthusiastic teachers on board. It is amazing when speaking to teachers in schools where the IWB hardware is in place but not being fully utilised, to discover that the boards were installed but the directive from the principal to actually use them was never formally made.

If the school principal (or school technology committee) has seen the value of IWB technology and is committed to moving forward with them, there is a good chance of succeeding. If they actually tell their teachers that they are expected to make the most of it, the chance of success is greater again. (If a principal really wants to send a strong signal to the staff about the IWB program, they should make sure they know how to use them themselves!) Getting strong support from the school leadership and winning over of a key majority of the staff to the educational value of the boards are a critical combination to making this work and starting out on the path to successful school-wide implementation.

Schools should not pretend that the challenge will necessarily be easy. And if a school happens to have either a principal who will not lead or is unwilling to draw the line in the sand and say 'this is the direction we are going', or a staff with an oversupply of technophobic teachers, then maybe the school is just not ready for IWBs yet. This would be an unfortunate situation for the students as they would be missing out on the many wonderful advantages that interactive technology can bring to their classrooms; but to insist on moving forward with IWBs when these two important elements for success are not in place would just lead to frustration and waste.

Bringing interactive technology to the school will almost certainly involve some adjustment to the way its teachers teach. If the school is serious about using IWBs, the first task should not be so much about deciding what type of board to buy, but to assess the likelihood of how well the teachers will make the cultural shift required to move towards this whole-school approach to an IWB-enabled classroom.

This sort of thinking flies in the face of what seems 'obvious' to the early adopters. To them, the advantages of this interactive technology seem so apparent, and many of them have trouble understanding why on earth everyone else cannot see it. 'If only these "Luddites" would get with the program!' they say. The inclination for the early adopter teachers is to just go ahead and do it anyway and hope the rest of the teachers will get more enthusiastic over time. What they sometimes fail to appreciate is that these other teachers are still the gatekeepers to what happens in their classrooms. And if the benefits are not immediately obvious to them, they will remain unconvinced that these new tools will improve the teaching and, even more importantly, the students' learning.

But perhaps we should not be quite so hard on these teachers. As educators, we know ourselves that if someone orders us to use a particular book or piece of technology or even a particular program and we do not believe in its educational benefit, we either will not use it or will simply make a half-hearted show of using it until the 'fad' passes. This is what happened with so many 'revolutionary' educational technologies over the years, many of which survived a short period of initial buzz that gradually faded away until they disappeared completely. (When was the last time you used an epidiascope? These fancy gadgets were all the rage in schools at one point, but you would be hard-pressed to find one today.) Many teachers—especially those who have been around for a while and seen these things come and go—are wary (and weary!) of hearing about 'the next big thing'. They have seen, sometimes over and over, many of these things flare up as the educational flavour-of-the-month, before quietly fading away to little more than a technological curiosity. Almost invariably, these technological changes were brought about when those on high decided something was a good idea, bought all the gear and then told the teachers to use it.

It is probably no surprise to discover that teachers who remain unconvinced of the educational worth of a new technology do not actively use that technology in their everyday teaching. To the eager tech-savvy teachers who just cannot wait to move forward with new technology, these 'laggards' are sometimes seen in a negative light as they appear to foil every step forward with their glass-is-half-empty mindset. Yet, although these teachers may be seen as the stumbling block to advancing with technology in the school, their perspectives can (if we allow them to have a voice) bring valuable insights to the process of ensuring the school's IWB implementation does not become yet another waste of time and money. They can even sometimes act as the voice of reason, forcing the more eager early adopters to temper their often unbridled enthusiasm and think through some of the logistical and practical issues of introducing IWBs across the school.

So if schools are to achieve a situation where all teachers are using IWBs as part of their everyday quality teaching, then the school leadership must address these issues at some point. If the less enthusiastic teachers are somehow not won over to the value that IWBs can bring to their classrooms, then this critical point of achieving whole-school acceptance will never be reached. What is now apparent in the work of the pathfinding IWB schools is that to get all teachers to accept the everyday use of any instructional technology, those teachers need to:

- believe their use of the technology will enhance their teaching and improve student learning
- feel comfortable using the technology
- be able to use the technology integrally in their everyday teaching

- have the technology readily available in each teaching room
- have tools that will also assist when required in the management and administration of their classes.

This is where leadership is required to open a few eyes (and sometimes minds) to what IWBs can actually offer, because the resistance is often borne of ignorance of what IWBs are actually all about. Most people who have seen an IWB being used well by a competent, experienced teacher would be hard-pressed to come up with a convincing argument that they would not enhance the teaching and learning process. Experience has repeatedly shown that the best way to gain acceptance of IWBs is to see them being used well by good teachers in real classroom settings. If a teacher has only ever taught in a conventional classroom it is difficult to explain the educational potential of interactive technology with words, writing or even the best of graphics. However, even the most sceptical observer starts to consider the possibilities for their own classroom when they watch a good teacher using a well set-up IWB to deliver an engaging lesson to students. Actually watching an IWB classroom in action, seeing the high engagement factor and the way the students interact with the technology will almost always convince any observer of their worth.

Often the worst person to sell the educational worth of an IWB is a salesperson who does not have a teaching background. It is amazing at times to see the useless features non-teachers try to promote. Salespeople often focus on the technological features of the hardware and software, rather than promoting ways in which IWBs can be used to supplement and enhance good-quality teaching. IWB marketing hype sometimes promotes the technology as a simple panacea for fixing schools, as though by adding them into our classrooms all our problems will magically disappear. They won't. Fortunately, more and more IWB vendors are making use of outstanding teachers to promote and demonstrate their products as well as do much of the initial training.

Hint: Do you want to whip up some enthusiasm for IWBs in your school? Rent a minibus for the day and take a load of your colleagues—including some of the less enthusiastic ones—off to a school already making good use of the boards and let them observe first-hand what good teaching in an IWB-enabled classroom is all about. Let them watch the way the students respond, ask questions of the teachers who use them every day, listen to how they are being used to create engaging digital lessons that can be shared and reused ... and you will be well on your way to a wider acceptance of their potential.

SEE AND DECIDE FOR YOURSELF

Arrange for a group from school to observe a good teacher teaching with an IWB—it does not matter whether it is a primary or secondary class. Each member of the group is then given a checklist that asks them to comment on the following areas.

1 What were the five main educational benefits you saw in the teacher's use of the IWB and associated teaching tools?
2 How do you feel the technology could have been better used?
3 What was it about the IWB that you think will appeal to all teachers, even those currently making little or no class use of digital technology?
4 What did you notice about the students' use of the technology?
5 Were there any particular ideas you picked up from the observation?
6 What kind of educational opportunities did you notice?
7 What other type of digital teaching tools would you like to have in your ideal classroom in addition to the IWB?
8 What particular issues will your school need to address if it moves ahead with IWBs throughout?

Take digital photos to show at the next staff meeting. Arrange for those who went on the visit to share their observations with the rest of the staff, and to identify their understanding of the key points for introducing and sustaining the effective use of IWBs. And remember, one can often learn as much from the shortcomings as from the strengths of such an experience.

Enthusiastic early adopters will often overcome huge obstacles to make the technology work with their students. By sheer force of will they will overcome logistical problems, invest inordinate amounts of their own time into learning new skills, put up with troublesome hardware issues, and generally roll up their sleeves to get the job done and make it work. For years it was thought that if one got a few of these early adopting teachers using the equipment, all the other teachers would follow. History has consistently demonstrated that this is not so.

So in summing up this chapter, to gain acceptance of interactive technology by all teachers in a school, you must have …

1 The right kind of leadership

The school needs a principal that is strong but not dictatorial, fully convinced of the benefits that IWBs will bring to their classrooms and shameless about their enthusiasm for the technology. Ideally the principal will have seen—and, hopefully, used—an IWB with students. Once the principal has a strong vision for what IWBs can bring to their school, they will be more likely to ensure that the inevitable hurdles and obstacles are overcome. Even in schools where decisions are made collaboratively by teams and committees, the principal is still the one who has the ultimate decision-making responsibility and so their importance to the success of an IWB program cannot be overstated. Get the principal on that minibus tour!

2 The right kind of training

The school must have an effective plan to bring the teachers up to speed with the necessary IWB skills. Every school is different, so it needs to make sure it comes up with a plan that works for all. Regular professional development, even something as simple as lunchtime show-and-tell sessions where teachers can share some of their success stories (and maybe even the not-so-successful stories) will help in getting the needed skills out to staff. Many IWB providers will freely supply their trainers to visit the school and run PD sessions.

An increasing number of schools are employing ICT integration specialists whose job it is to work with teachers to help with technology in the classroom, but even in schools that do not have this luxury the school boards and district offices will usually offer some sort of regular IWB training at very minimal cost. Making IWB professional development a regular part of staff meetings and PD days is an obvious thing to do, especially if the school has made a big financial commitment to IWB technology. Training is certainly a key factor in getting the most from the school's IWB investment, and access to this training needs to be as frictionless and freely available as possible.

And remember the key role that quality teaching plays in all of this. If a teacher is struggling to be effective with technology, help them by ensuring they understand the key components of sound pedagogy—student-centred learning, authentic tasks, effective dialogue, quality teaching methods and so on. These are foundational understandings to an effective classroom environment and no amount of professional development in using IWBs will help if those skills are being applied on top of poor teaching methods.

Either way, training is important. It is easy to talk about how the school is using technology, but when it comes right down to it, it is about the PD, not the PR.

3   The right technology investment

Quality products, well installed, will go a long way to ensuring that the school achieves the greatest acceptance of and best use from their IWBs. Remember that quality is remembered long after price is forgotten. If the teachers can walk into a room and just KNOW that everything will work as planned, this factor alone will win over many of the sceptical hearts and minds. Technology that is flaky, breaks down or is hard to use will never gain acceptance by all teachers and will always be cited as the reason for not using it.

Make it easy to use and make sure it works all the time. Think about the way the teachers will use the IWBs and design their implementation accordingly. Some of the practical aspects of this are discussed in the next chapter, but it is important to get this part right.

4   Plenty of patience

You may think that the shift to better learning will start to happen as soon as the new boards are installed in the school, but it is probably going to take a little longer than that—and a fair amount of patience. After all, it may be the start of a shift towards a whole new culture for learning and teaching in the school. Changing an entrenched culture is never an easy process and nowhere is this truer than in schools. The end goal is to have quality whole-school adoption of IWB technology in a seamlessly integrated way, but it will take time and everyone needs to be aware of this from the outset.

As well as being patient as this shift is made, at the same time you ought to remain focused on the big picture and maintain the pressure to keep this cultural change moving over an extended period of time. Maybe the school is different and a quick and seamless transition to this digital classroom culture is achievable, but in all likelihood it may take several years to truly shift the underlying culture and get all the teachers 'thinking digitally'. However long it takes, remember that there must be the willingness to lead people from where they are to where they need to be, and the patience to make it happen.

If you can get this balance right, the school will be well on its way to success.

CHAPTER **3**

SETTING UP YOUR CLASSROOM

This chapter will explore some of the technical issues around the choice, installation and use of interactive technologies for your school. But first, a word of caution. The real challenges to be overcome in the move towards an interactive teaching and learning environment are not technological, but cultural. The work is not about understanding the technical factors nearly as much as it is about developing a new mindset about changing your teaching to take advantage of the new possibilities that IWBs offer. If you are to get successful whole-school integration of interactive technologies, you will ultimately spend less time on the 'how' and more time on the 'why'.

But for the moment, let us assume you have accepted the notion that adopting the widespread use of IWBs is more an exercise in culture shifting than it is about technology per se. And let us assume also that you have supportive leadership willing to commit to a realistic and achievable plan of funding and professional development. With these basic understandings in place, it is true that you will need to spend some time thinking about the hardware and software issues surrounding IWBs.

CHOOSING THE RIGHT TECHNOLOGY

The normal first step is to start thinking which board you should buy. The marketplace for interactive whiteboards has become highly competitive over the last few years and there are a large number of IWB hardware vendors eager for your business. This is great news for schools as it offers some real choice and puts them in a good bargaining position, especially if buying a number of boards and the associated bits and pieces such as voting systems. It can also be confusing for some as they attempt to cut through the marketing hype and make informed decisions about the significant money they are about to spend.

In this section we will look at the various IWB technologies available, some of their strengths and weaknesses, considerations to bear in mind about how they are installed in the classrooms, and some tips for keeping them working well.

When browsing through the archives of any educational mailing lists or technology blogs, one finds plenty of questions posted there asking for advice on which brand of board to buy. Of course, we all want to make sure we make the right decisions before we spend the cash, but there is this curious idea that if we simply buy the best equipment—be it the best TV, the best video, the best computers or even the best textbooks—then the quality of the technology will somehow improve the quality of the teaching. While it would be comforting to think that simply having the best equipment will be a recipe for instant success, there is far more to it than this. By all means, do the research in order to get the right technology for the school, but remember that this is just one small part of the overall picture. It is—and always has been—the quality of teaching throughout the school that makes the real difference to student learning, not the brand or type of technology.

An innovative, creative and technically adept teacher using a cheaper, 'no name' brand of IWB will always get better results than a conservative, 'Luddite-ish' teacher using the latest and greatest IWB from the leading manufacturer. The focus from the outset should be on enriching the teaching that takes place within the classrooms and securing whole-staff acceptance of the technology. These are both far bigger factors for success than the specific choice of technology.

THE BOARDS ON OFFER

While they might seem like magic the first time you see an interactive whiteboard being used well, it is in essence nothing more than a large, touch-screen track-pad that enables a teacher to control a computer remotely using a pen or finger. This concept might seem simple enough, but almost every demonstration to new IWB users seems to invoke the same predictable 'Can the IWB do this/Can the IWB do that?' type of questions, to which the answer is generally: 'If you can do it on your computer, you can do it on the IWB'. On first appearances, it looks like the IWB is doing the work, but it is not. The IWB just drives the computer … simple as that. While the idea of being able to project a large screen image at the front of the classroom, enabling the display of and interaction with all manner of engaging digital content, certainly opens up a plethora of possibilities in any classroom, remember that all that the teacher is doing is driving the computer using the board. So if the computer can do it, the IWB can do it.

The history of the IWB differs in several significant ways from all the previous instructional technologies used by schools. As mentioned in Chapter 1, perhaps the most significant factor is that IWBs were designed from the outset for teacher use; they were not designed for the general consumer or office markets like so many other technologies that educators had to adapt for classroom use. As IWB technology gathered momentum in the early part of the twenty-first century, different manufacturers used fundamentally different underlying technologies, and hence came up with different ways of creating an 'interactive whiteboard'. Right from the beginning there was no real coordinated effort to adopt an industry standard for the way IWBs were created. While all the various technological approaches to building an IWB work fine, each has certain pros and cons that ought to be taken into account. These different approaches are not inherently better or worse than each other, but they have given rise to a sort of VHS-versus-Beta situation and carry implications for which IWB technology may be the right one for your particular situation.

The vast majority of the IWBs used in schools are what is known as front-projection boards. In time, that situation could change as the cost of alternative technologies drops, but at the time of writing front-projection IWBs are appreciably cheaper than the other types; and when you are equipping a whole school, price matters. With a front-projection IWB there is the need for a board, a data projector projecting onto the board, a computer, and a carefully calibrated relationship between the data projector and the board. With that calibration, students and teachers are able to work the board using their finger or a stylus, in the same way they would work with a mouse on a computer monitor.

Boards vary in size and shape. The trend is towards the larger size, with around 72-inch being regarded as standard. Boards are available in both a standard 4:3 or a wide-screen 16:9 format, and although the 4:3 format is still most common, as newer computers and projectors come on the market that are capable of running in 16:9 format there will probably be a trend towards the wide-screen ratio. Either combination works fine, but you should aim to match your computer, projector and interactive board to all take advantage of whatever format you choose. For example, although projecting a newer wide-screen (16:9) computer though an older 4:3 projector onto a 4:3 board will work, it will require some re-sizing on the computer's screen. This can be a nuisance for teachers who stay connected to their IWB all day and are forced to stare at a slightly fuzzy and stretched screen running in a non-native resolution. Note: The smaller (and cheaper) boards should only be considered for use in seminar rooms or with very young students who struggle to reach the controls on the larger boards.

The computer that drives the board also serves as the control for access to all the other digital facilities, be it the network, the Internet, digital television, sound systems or the many other facilities within the digital toolkit, so it needs to be up to whatever demands may be placed upon it.

There are several types of IWB technology, with the two main ones being resistive membrane and electromagnetic pickup. Some are still quite experimental, but all point to an interesting future. Following is an overview of the various IWB technologies available.

Analogue resistive membrane technology

This is often also referred to as a 'soft' board. Originally pioneered by the Canadian-based SMART Technologies for their SMART Board products, this technology is also used by companies like Egan Teamboard, Polyvision and Panasonic.

With softboard technology, the basic principle is that the outer surface of the board—the part you 'write' on—is separated from the supporting backboard by a thin layer of air. These types of boards have a slight springy feel when touched, hence the term 'softboard'. When pressed using a pen or finger, the two slightly separated surfaces come into contact with each other to register a 'touch' and the fine mesh of contact points that is spread between the layers accurately translates the pressure applied to the outer surface of the board into a specific pixel point on the screen of the computer.

Those who use soft IWB technology say its major attraction is the ability to interact with the board using any object, including a finger. Being able to touch the surface with a finger gives the softboard a wonderfully tactile nature and is great encouragement for students—

especially younger students—to interact directly with it. Apart from the slight springy feel, the writing surface of these boards is generally similar to the white, low-friction surfaces of regular, non-interactive whiteboards. (It is best not to actually write on them, though; regardless of the type of technology, most IWB makers do not recommend writing on them with regular marker pens.)

For those times when a finger may not be the ideal pointing device, a stylus pen can also be used on the softboard. Just as a finger would, the stylus registers a series of pressure points as it drags across the surface of the IWB and the software follows these pressure points, giving the effect of writing on the board using digital ink. Teachers and students can therefore write on the board in much the same way that a regular board can be written on; although at this stage in the development of this technology the board still behaves mostly in a single-touch mode and allows only one point of contact. For anyone used to resting the side of their hand on a traditional whiteboard as they write, this single-touch mode means they must modify their writing technique to avoid touching the board's surface, since the pen tip is the only contact point allowed.

Worth noting is that some softboard vendors, such as SMART Technology, also offer rear-projection boards where the projector is mounted internally so no shadows are cast by users as they stand in front of the board. At this stage, these boards are considerably more expensive than their front-projection counterparts.

One of the problems often encountered by new users of softboard technology is a fear of pressing too hard and damaging the board's surface. They tend to press too lightly as they drag over the surface, usually causing the board to not register the touch correctly, causing objects to skip unpredictably or broken lines to be drawn in place of continuous ones. Don't be afraid to press firmly!

Despite the somewhat misleading term 'softboard', this technology is still very robust and the word 'soft' should not be construed to suggest any lack of durability.

Electromagnetic pickup technology

These types of IWB are known as 'hard' boards, so called because their outer surface is a hard, flat layer, similar in rigidity and general feel to the solid surface of a regular whiteboard. This technology was developed by companies like Numonics in the US and Promethean in the UK.

The electromagnetic pickup technology works by passing a special electronic stylus pen across the surface of the board, which activates an electronic grid of sensors embedded into the board as it moves over them. The stylus pen is required for using the board, so other objects such as fingers cannot be used to interact with these board types. The stylus has a pressure-sensitive tip, so the experience is very much like writing on a regular board with a regular pen but with the ability to click, double-click or drag objects on the screen by tapping on the tip of the pen. Because the board is only picking up the tip of the special pen, no touch is registered by any other contact points such as a hand or finger, and this means that while hardboard technology cannot be used with a finger, it does allow for resting of the hand on the surface while writing. For many people this feels like a far more natural way of writing.

One big advantage of hardboard technology is that, because the pen may be moved across the surface of the board without registering an actual click, software features based on a standard 'mouse-over' action still work as expected. This mouse-over concept is common to many software applications, including web browsers that will display 'alt text' as you hover over a link or image, or the 'tool tips' such as those found in Microsoft Office, where a tool will pop up a short description of its function without the need to actually click it. (By contrast, mouse-overs do not work on most softboards; soft technology requires actual pen contact to take place so are therefore unaware of a pen hovering over the button until it actually registers a touch.)

One potential issue with the hardboard is the need to have a special stylus pen for it to work. If you lose the pen, the board cannot function. In many schools where classroom theft is an issue, pens cannot be left in the room with the board so the teacher must carry the pens from class to class. Apart from the inconvenience if a teacher happens to forget the stylus pen, a hardboard often has improved levels of accuracy if it is paired up with the same pen all the time. Of course, any pen will work, but to get proper accuracy the pen may need to be recalibrated a couple of times to create this accurate pairing.

OTHER TYPES OF IWB TECHNOLOGIES

Interactive whiteboards are experiencing the same rapid development as all other digital technologies, so what form they will take ten years from now is hard to tell. What is clear, however, is that today's interactive boards are likely to last appreciably longer than the personal computers or data projectors that drive them. While the computers and projectors will need to be updated every three to four years, the lifespan of the boards should be considerably longer. This longevity is a good thing and does not suggest obsolescence as major updates and improvements are generally software-based and do not involve the actual boards.

What we do know is that all instructional technology will move through a life cycle, and ultimately disappear into the museum. As an example, think about the life cycle of the audio cassette or CD-ROM, both of which are essentially obsolete technologies now being replaced by DVD and BluRay disks. Having said that, teaching-board technology— even in the form of the humble blackboard—has had a life cycle of over two centuries and is still being used, so this suggests that the IWB, conceptually at least, has a lot of life left in it yet.

Although the great majority of IWBs fall into the previous two categories of front-projection hardboards and softboards, there are also a number of alternative and emerging technologies that could meet your IWB needs, such as Ultrasonic Tracking and Infrared Tracking.

Ultrasonic Tracking technology

Ultrasonic Tracking technology was developed by Virtual Ink, a Boston-based dotcom and is currently marketed in such products as the Mimio board (www.mimio.com) and the eBeam (www.e-beam.com). Ultrasonic technology has a distinct advantage of being able to turn any regular whiteboard into an interactive surface and, although it requires special pen holders and styluses, might be an interesting option for schools looking to introduce interactive technologies without the costs and installation requirements of more conventional IWBs.

Ultrasonic Tracking works by having two ultrasonic microphones bouncing high-frequency sound waves across the surface of the board, listening for the bounce-back from the stylus and measuring the difference in the sound's arrival time. It then triangulates the location of the stylus on the board. Although it may sound like voodoo to the non-technical, these systems can be surprisingly accurate. Controls for the system are located within the ultrasonic sending unit, which normally attaches to the side or corner of a regular dry-erase whiteboard. Using a special pen holder, these technologies can also act as a tool for digitally capturing whatever is written on the conventional boards using regular dry-erase whiteboard markers.

Infrared Tracking technology

Infrared Tracking technology is another interesting alternative found in the range of Onfinity products made by the Ontech Group. The Onfinity (www.onfinity.com) is a small tracking device that can be pointed at any surface and scans across it with an infrared signal. When hooked to a computer and calibrated to the projected image, it is then able to treat that image as an interactive surface. Like ultrasonic technology, Infrared requires no special surface, making it an interesting option for turning regular surfaces into interactive ones.

One downside of the infrared technology is that the send/receive unit requires a clear view of the board in order to maintain a continual scan of the surface. This can be problematic as teachers and students interact with the board, and it is easy to experience dropouts in the signal as the users get between the board and the unit. Still, in certain situations it is a technology with some promise.

AND BEYOND ...

Other technologies currently exist that, although still in a relatively experimental stage, offer some interesting possibilities for the future and are worth mentioning briefly.

- **Plasma Overlay technology** is yet another method of creating an interactive surface. It involves placing a touch-sensitive glass panel over a regular large plasma or LCD screen. The main advantage is the elimination of the projector and the ability to create interactive panels in a range of different sizes. An example of this technology is the overlay screens made by Next Window (www.nextwindow.com) that work on a variety of screens as well as plain walls. For classroom use the cost is still prohibitive, especially for screens that compare with the size of current IWBs, but like all technologies the cost will probably come down eventually.

- **Multi-touch technology** was pioneered by Jeff Han and has amazing possibilities for creating large touch-sensitive screens that can be interacted with using multiple touch points. Video footage of Han demonstrating the device went viral on YouTube during 2007 and his research has been spun off into a company called Perceptive Pixel (www.perceptivepixel.com). It remains to be seen how feasible and affordable this technology may be for classrooms, but there is no doubt that it offers some stunning possibilities for the future of IWBs.

- **The Philips Entertaible** was an interesting development in 2006 by the Dutch electronics company Philips in consultation with UK teacher Tom Barrett. Tom was invited by Philips to offer an educational perspective on the development of the technology, and he documents his experiences with the Entertaible project on his blog (http://tbarrett.edublogs.org/2008/11/08/multi-touch-interactive-desk-from-durham-university/). The Entertaible technology was also used in research being done at Durham University in the UK. This research, called SynergyNet, focused on investigating alternative forms that interactive technology could take and especially how it could assist with developing social pedagogies. The notion of taking an interactive surface and making it horizontal like a desk—rather than vertical like a wall—is a fascinating one. Certainly, using a table concept and embedding a flat, interactive, multi-touch surface into it opens up a whole range of possibilities in the classroom that focus squarely on the learners. It reinforces the idea that the world of interactive technologies is still young and there are many ideas and applications yet to be explored in the coming years.

- **Microsoft Surface technology** first appeared in late 2007 in the form of a multi-touch table. Using a series of cameras and optics, the Microsoft Surface technology (www.microsoft.com/surface) offers an interactive flat surface that can be drawn on, touched, clicked and dragged. Early demonstrations showed the interactive table surface interfacing directly with mobile phones, credit cards and digital cameras, and suggest that touch-based interfaces could be used to solve many complex problems in areas from hospitality to tourism. In 2008, Microsoft demonstrated a vertical version of the Surface technology, effectively creating a large multi-touch IWB screen. Pricing on the Surface technology is still prohibitive for large-scale use in education, but it has fascinating potential.

- **The SMART Table** is another product that takes an interactive, multi-touch surface and sets it horizontally into a table-like form. Canadian IWB manufacturer SMART Technology released the product in late 2008, and it will be interesting to see where this technology goes now that it is in full commercial production from one of the biggest names in interactive technology. The fact that it comes from a company like SMART lends a good deal of legitimacy to the interactive table concept, although the price tag probably still puts it out of reach for large-scale, school-wide deployment. Hopefully the prices will drop over time to make it more affordable, but it is interesting that we now have an actual multi-touch table product in production, which only a couple of years ago was barely more than an interesting concept. This kind of rapid evolution is typical of the dynamic nature of the interactive technologies market.

- **The Wii Remote IWB:** In early 2008, another video appeared on YouTube that suggested some interesting possibilities for the future of interactive technologies. A young man by the name of Johnny Chung Lee took a simple ballpoint pen, replaced its innards with an infrared LED and managed to hook it up to a Nintendo Wii Remote device. The end result was the ability to turn any surface into an interactive, multi-touch response system for about $55. Although these early 'Wiimote' systems were somewhat primitive and lacked polish, the idea was picked up by a scattered group of global open-source hackers who have worked hard at refining and developing the original idea into a far more polished concept. Since then the technology has moved ahead rapidly and, along with the development of specialised driver software called Smoothboard, it is now approaching a point where it presents a credible alternative to commercial IWBs. The Wiimote IWB is being developed as an open-source hardware project, with all the technological advancements being openly documented for anyone to emulate. Much of this global development is coordinated through a collaborative development group called the Wiimote Project, headed by Ben Jones from Australia and Goh Boon Jin from Singapore.

   For those keen to learn more about the technology, the most comprehensive site for information about setting up your own Wiimote IWB can be found at http://www.boonjin.com/smoothboard.

Clearly, some of these technologies are in the early stages of development for commercial use and some are still a long way from prime-time use in classrooms. However, they highlight the fact that dynamic changes are taking place in the interactive technologies space and hint that we are in for some exciting times ahead. Regardless of how IWBs may or may not evolve for the classrooms of the future, it is important to remember that it is not about the type of technology but rather the type of teaching behind it. A good teacher, teaching with sound methods that take full advantage of the interactive potential, is always going to be a more important ingredient for success than any particular technology, no matter how magical it may appear to be.

As tempting as it may be to be dazzled by what lies out on the horizon, you should bear in mind that at this point in history all of the current commercially available technologies work well and provide teachers with a simple-to-use, highly reliable and—when used to support good-quality teaching—immensely powerful technology.

THE MAGIC IS IN THE SOFTWARE

Of course, the real effectiveness of IWB technology is only partly to do with the hardware. The power of good hardware is amplified by the addition of specialised software that gives extra functionality to the board. As well as the basic driver software that lets the computer communicate with the IWB, this specialised software is usually in the form of 'notebook' or 'flipchart' software that behaves a little like Microsoft PowerPoint but with additional functionality, including the ability to let you drag objects around the screen freely. Although this sounds like a minor distinction, the ability to freely drag objects around a large shared screen forms a core feature of the IWB experience. When we watch an IWB user working with a board, much of the interactivity we see is based around this idea of being able to easily drag movable objects around the screen. There are other important IWB-specific features built into the software, too, including a variety of virtual pens and highlighting tools useful for magnifying and focusing on parts of a page, as well as easy access to a large collection of images, backgrounds and interactive tools. These may sound like simple features but they are central to building an effective IWB experience and are not found in most other software applications, or at least not in the same integrated way.

As you think about what board will best meet your needs, keep in mind that the real magic is in the software, not the hardware.

Although the software is the real heart of an IWB system, there is still a surprising lack of standardisation between the various IWB vendors. Interactive whiteboard software made by one company is not generally directly compatible with interactive software produced by another company, meaning that a lesson prepared in one system is not always able to be easily (or legally) used with a competitor's product. Many IWB manufacturers realise all too well that their software is usually the key differentiator of their products and do not seem too interested in adhering to a standard format that will allow lessons prepared in their application to be easily shared with their competitor's product. Even with the number of different proprietary formats for IWB software, there is precious little effort being given to making the resources created with one brand of IWB software work easily on a different type of board hardware.

This can have implications for employment options, with increasing numbers of teachers who have experience using one brand of board keen to work in schools that have the same type of board; if a teacher has been teaching with one brand for a couple of years and has developed a large personal collection of resources and lessons for that brand of board, moving to a new school that uses a different brand can be a big decision! This lack of compatibility between brands means that the many hours of work put into developing teaching resources for a particular brand of board will render them unusable at the new school. Even now, there are growing numbers of teachers whose first question at the job interview is 'What brand of IWB do you use?' For some teachers, hearing that the new school uses a different brand of IWB means they might as well end the interview right there unless they are willing to recreate all their lessons in the new format.

Thankfully the situation is starting to improve. For example, the latest version of Promethean's ActivInspire software now has built-in converters to open interactive lesson files created by their main competitor, Smart Notebook.

While this book aims to be as agnostic as possible to specific brands of boards, it would be hard to have this conversation without at least acknowledging the dominance at this point in time of the two major players in the IWB business—SMART and Promethean—and thinking about how their dominance might affect the way other IWB software evolves. Between them, SMART Notebook and Promethean ActivInspire and ActivStudio hold a significant share of the IWB software market. There are probably valid reasons for this current dominance as both SMART and Promethean were pioneers in the field and made an early commitment to the education sector. They are both relatively mature, stable products with strong company support, but still more importantly they have a huge community of users who all share resources freely via an online marketplace. While there is limited compatibility between brands, the value of this online community of users should continue to be a major factor in any evaluation of an IWB product. So, to continue the VHS-versus-Beta analogy, you do not want to be the one using Beta if everyone else is using VHS.

It has been interesting to watch the development of features leapfrog past each other in every new version of IWB software from the major players. In any relatively immature market, much innovation and competition are constantly taking place, and this is certainly the case with IWB software development. As one vendor releases a new software version with great new features, it often compels their competitors to not only match but exceed those features in their next update. For example, ActivStudio 3 was released with new features called 'actions', 'restrictors' and 'containers' that were not present in version 2. Using these new features, teachers could build a greater level of interactivity into lessons, defining how specific objects reacted to clicks and taps on the board, limiting their movement to predefined paths or positions and predefining how objects interacted with each other. Similar features were not available in SMART Notebook 9.7, and for a while it appeared that ActivStudio users had the upper hand. However, the latest release of SMART Notebook 10 saw the introduction of a whole array of new animation features that now offer similar possibilities for SMART Board users, as well as a bunch of other usable features such as windowshades on individual table cells. Shortly before this book went to press, Promethean released ActivInspire, the much anticipated update to ActivStudio. ActivInspire was developed with an entirely new codebase, based on extensive consultation and suggestions from teachers all over the world, and was rebuilt from the ground up to provide greater usability and better integration of various multimedia types. Significantly, Promethean revised the licence terms to allow anybody to download and install the software, regardless of whether they were the owner of a Promethean IWB or not. In a bold move, they also declared that ActivInspire was able to be used on any hardware, permitting owners of any brand of IWB to use their software.

Other notable players exist in the marketplace, such as Interwrite with their Workbook application. It contains many of the same features as the SMART and Promethean products, and although the files it produces are not compatible with these other brands, there is a remarkable similarity in the overall look and feel of the product. It has a few features not supported by its competitors, and is lacking a few that their competitors do have, although there are indications that the missing features will appear in future versions of the software.

This sort of cat-and-mouse game supports the idea that IWB software is still in a fairly early stage of maturity, and the notion of a 'standard' IWB feature set is still being worked out. One would imagine that as this type of software matures over the next few years, the marketplace will ultimately decide which features should be core components of interactive software and which should not. If the IWB software market evolves in the same way that most other software markets have, all vendors will gradually converge on a set of relatively standard features that work in essentially the same way, with greater compatibility (or at least some degree of reliable interoperability) between them.

The ideal solution would seem to be a universally available software application that could be used on all boards, regardless of brand. This is the idea behind the Easiteach product, which aims to be a stand-alone, hardware-agnostic IWB environment that can be used on any board. Easiteach is certainly gaining traction in some schools although it does not appear to be a real threat to either of the two leading brands as yet (http://www.easiteach.com/).

Another interesting hardware-independent option is the Open Whiteboard Project, an open-source software project originally proposed by Swedish web developer Johan Kohlin. Kohlin, who teaches at Jönköping University in Sweden, commenced work on the project himself, although he is currently looking for other developers to collaborate with. The Open Whiteboard Project aims to build a completely free and open IWB application for use on any IWB as an alternative to the commercial products. More information can be found at http://sourceforge.net/projects/openwhiteboard/.

In an effort to achieve some degree of standardisation, the UK-based educational technology organisation Becta initiated work in 2007 that aims to provide a set of standards to build IWB software that will transfer material from one vendor's product to another (http://tinyurl.com/2etdlm/). This two-phase development, overseen by the RM technology group, will start by defining a common set of software specifications and eventually publish the source code for a viewer that will open any type of IWB software. It is a bold initiative that could, if they manage to pull it off, make life a lot simpler for teachers who wish to share resources from one board to another.

This standardisation of IWB software formats would be a useful thing, although one could also argue that any attempt to put limits or standards on what IWB software should be able to do will make it harder for individual manufacturers to be innovative and add new features.

Time will tell just how this all pans out, but regardless of whether we manage to get some standardisation across the industry, at this point in time it is probably still best to plan on the assumption that the boards are not compatible and at the very least ought not to be mixed within the one school.

In conclusion

Give some thought to the software that comes with the board. The most important aspect to consider with any board is the quality of the teaching software provided. You will want a comprehensive suite of digital teaching applications that can cater for highly sophisticated users —both teachers and students. Do not buy something aimed too much at just beginning users, for within a year both the teachers and the students will want more sophisticated software that allows them to constantly push the envelope.

'Macintosh' schools need to ensure that they select a board that comes with quality Mac teaching software. Most of the leading brands have software that comes in both Windows and Macintosh versions, and some even support Linux. With the cheaper end of the market, check the functionality of the Mac version, as some vendors have some way to go with their Mac software refinement before Apple users will be happy.

Do an in-depth test of the various teaching software options before buying. It is very difficult to change your mind about the boards across the school once you are underway. Either undertake that in-depth testing yourself, or rely on the word of a trusted expert teacher who has explored the many features of the teaching software. Do not rely on the salesperson. Their job is ultimately to sell boards and not necessarily to provide an even-handed comparison of the various offerings.

Regardless of brand, the leading IWB software is already very sophisticated. All of the offerings are likely to 'wow' the first-time user. It is therefore important to explore each of the offerings in depth and to recognise which of the offerings will meet the school's needs. Take advantage of the facility to download demo versions of teaching software from each vendor's website and try it out. Be wary of any vendor not willing to provide a trial copy of their teaching software.

INSTALLATION POINTS TO CONSIDER

Avoid portable boards

This might seem obvious, but the boards should be mounted permanently on the classroom walls. Some schools have attempted to go with portable IWBs on movable trolleys, but this is generally a recipe for failure. The underlying rationale behind wanting portable boards usually sounds good, and at first glance the reasons seem valid enough …

- 'We can only afford a few boards at this stage, so we want to be able to move them around.'
- 'We want to be more equitable in the way we share the boards between different classrooms.'
- 'We think that having portable boards will save money on installation costs.'
- 'We're worried about potential vandalism, so we want to be able to lock them away when not being used.'

The truth is that portable boards are hard to move around, time-consuming to set up and frustrating to use; they steal valuable class time with the constant setting up and pulling down of a data projector; they are inconvenient; they require constant recalibration; and they are far more likely to get damaged. Having to fiddle around with power leads and projectors in order to use the board is simply not a viable proposition for most teachers, and while a few diehard technology buffs might be prepared to do that, the vast majority of teachers will not.

This is why mobile IWBs simply do not work in the long term—teachers will not use them if they constantly steal precious time away from the lesson. Although having movable IWBs may seem like a good solution for schools that are introducing the technology and want to share them around the school in an equitable way, the truth is that this approach rarely succeeds and the boards never really build enough critical mass to be used well. Accept the reality of mounting your IWB permanently in your classroom. All the conventional wisdom—and lots of research—suggests that IWBs must be permanently installed into classrooms to be effective in the long term.

The only time a portable board might make sense is when a school already has a strong commitment to IWBs but perhaps wants a movable board to be used at staff meetings, parent nights, training sessions or other such events. In such cases, a portable board can be a valuable piece of equipment. For all other situations, however, a portable board should never be seen as the primary means of bringing IWB technology into a school.

Burn the boats

Teachers will get the most benefit out of an interactive whiteboard if its use is seamlessly integrated into their daily routine. While they may not necessarily want to use their IWB every minute of the day, the ideal situation is such that they can access it on demand when they want it.

If the IWB is to become the primary tool for bringing digital resources into the classroom, it belongs in a place where everyone can see it.

In many schools about to make a serious commitment to IWB technology, teachers will have passionate discussions about whether the interactive whiteboard should completely replace the existing conventional teaching boards. The argument is made that teachers still need the conventional board; they still need a place to write notes; and they don't want to have to use an IWB all the time. Listen carefully to these discussions. They will give an insight into just how much of a culture shift the school is about to face—whether teachers enthusiastically agree to get rid of the old boards and replace them with an IWB; whether they argue tooth and nail that the existing boards should stay and the IWBs should go 'to the side'. Some may even suggest that the IWB be mounted on the back wall … 'That gives us the best of both worlds; we still have the regular whiteboard at the front of the room and the students just need to turn around to see the IWB when we use it.' (Yes, this sort of thinking really does exist in some schools.) Needless to say, if the decision is made to mount IWBs to the side or even at the back of classrooms, this could be a warning sign that the school is likely to be facing rather more of a culture shift than they are prepared for. In these discussions about where the boards should go, the degree of resistance that arises can provide an interesting insight into the underlying mindsets about IWBs and the challenges likely to be faced as the school tries to move towards a new type of digital teaching.

That is not to say that tearing down the old whiteboards (or blackboards) and having only an IWB is necessarily the right solution for your school. There may be perfectly valid reasons for maintaining some access to conventional boards, and a well-made case by teachers should be listened to and judged on its merit. In some high school classrooms, especially, having some conventional whiteboard space can be a very handy thing, useful for jotting down a quick note when the projector has been turned off, or for many other practical reasons. Conventional boards are also useful when substitute or casual teachers have to take a class as they may not be skilled in the use of IWBs.

Some schools do rip all the old boards out; some keep a bit of conventional board space just in case; and some treat the IWBs as something they plan to use only occasionally. And while there is no right or wrong answer, you ought to be aware that the decisions you make about where you place your IWBs are reflective of other, deeper issues of organisational change. There is no point hedging your bets about installing IWBs in your classrooms and then complaining that teachers are not making the most of them. If they have an option between using the new technology or sticking to the old ways with which they feel more comfortable, it should come as no surprise that the IWBs will take much longer to have any real effect.

As you consider which installation strategy you will use for your boards, you might like to ponder the following tale: In the early 1500s, the great conquistador Hernan Cortez invaded Mexico. As his men landed on the Mexican shores and prepared for battle, Cortez issued a command to burn the boats they arrived in. His men were shocked—with no means of getting back to their native land they realised that their only chance of survival was to fight and win. As drastic as it seemed, burning the boats was an act of total commitment to their long-term success. If you are serious about setting yourself up for success with IWBs, if you really want to let go of the old ways and move into the brave new world of digital schooling, you have to let go of some of the things that are anchoring you to the past.

So, if you want to make interactive technologies a truly embedded part of the way your school operates, maybe it is time to 'burn your boats'. Maybe you should get the biggest IWB you can and mount it front and centre. Maybe you should get rid of the old boards completely. Because if you cling to the old ways of doing things, keeping your old boards and trying to compromise and justify that you still need them, there is a good chance that three years down the track you will still be struggling with a culture shift that just won't budge and wondering where the return is on all this investment.

Design it for student use

One of the giveaways that IWB technology has been put in place with the teachers in mind rather than the students is when boards get installed at 'grown-up' level. If IWB technology really is about the students using it as well as the teachers, then mounting the boards at a suitable height is very important.

For the very young students, the boards need to be set at a level where they can access them easily. We all know that kindergarten kids are only little, and yet something as seemingly obvious as mounting the boards at child-friendly heights seems to escape the attention of many IWB installations. It is not unreasonable for the base of a kindergarten IWB to be no more than 30–40 centimetres from the floor. There are also accessories available for some boards that can help make it easy for the smaller students, such as stylus pens in the form of long wands that help the students have greater reach on the boards, even when they are mounted low.

Designing for student use means maintaining easy access for students at all time. Of course, as the students get older, the corresponding mounted height of the board needs to increase to suit their size.

Clear the clutter

One thing that becomes obvious very quickly when starting to use a typical interactive whiteboard is the shadow cast by the user on the writing surface. Because of the way the projector throws light at the board, users' writing technique needs to be modified slightly or they will find themselves constantly getting in their own shadow and unable to see what they are doing.

As you change your board technique to accommodate this, you will probably find yourself standing to one side or the other and reaching into the board space, rather than standing directly in front of it. Given that this technique of standing to one side is a necessity in order to stay out of your own shadow, it is amazing to see boards installed into classrooms where the amount of space allocated to the board is just as wide as the board itself, and the spaces to the side of the board are taken up with cupboards, shelves, tables and so on. Arranging furniture on either side of the board may seem very efficient until you start using the board—you will soon realise just how impractical it really is.

So get rid of any clutter and maintain a wide, clear space on either side of the board to allow both you and your students to move out of the projected shadow while interacting with the board.

Have the job done by a professional

Mounting an IWB looks easy. It would seem that anyone who can use a drill and a screwdriver could do it, and some schools may decide to save a few dollars by getting their local handyman to mount them. In the long run, however, this is probably false economy.

There is more to mounting an IWB than might first be apparent, and having some specialised knowledge can make a big difference.

Knowledge of optimum lengths for cable runs, correct placement of powered USB boosters, thorough testing of VGA cabling for signal strength, hooking into a clean power supply, getting the ideal arrangements of speakers, input panels, etc. all contribute to a successful and trouble-free IWB installation.

So it is best to get the job done by a professional installer who has a strong track record with the particular brand of board. Ask for references from other clients and, if possible, take a look at the installer's workmanship in other schools. Remember that IWBs are quite robust pieces of technology and that nearly all future problems that may be experienced will probably come down to the quality of the installation job. Taking the cheapest quote may not always be the cheapest option in the long run.

If you are planning on getting a number of boards installed, it may be worthwhile getting them installed at the same time. There may be some economies of scale to be had by getting many of the cabling and electrical jobs done while the installers are on the school premises. The per-board installation costs are likely to be lower if the installers are doing a number of boards at the same time.

Installation checklist

- Interactive whiteboard, mounted in an appropriate position and height
- Data projector (either mounted on the ceiling or on a short arm suspended above the board)
- Speakers mounted on the wall on either side of the board
- Volume control for the audio
- Power supply for the IWB, audio, computer and associated peripherals
- Cabling for power, USB, audio and projector
- Housing for desktop computer, or place to plug in a laptop computer
- Ideally, some form of switching interface for connecting other devices to the IWB such as DVD or VHS players, document cameras, CD players, radios, iPods, gaming consoles, etc.

A FEW MORE THOUGHTS ABOUT MAKING THE RIGHT IWB DECISION

Select the one board for use throughout the school, and stick to it. As mentioned, IWBs are not totally compatible and having more than one brand in a school is a recipe for confusion. Apart from the multiple training and support requirements, the other major problem is the difficulty in transferring lesson files from one brand of board to another. It can be messy and inconvenient.

Discuss with the IWB providers the likely life of the school's investment and the options for having the functionality of the board consistently enhanced. For example, can your existing boards be upgraded to multi-touch technology when it hits the market? It ought to be something that can be done relatively easily (and cheaply) with a simple firmware upgrade.

How often should the school be prepared to replace the boards? Certainly, an IWB should far outlive the typical three-year life cycle of a personal computer, but do not expect that your IWBs will last forever. Like all technology, they will eventually become obsolete and will need updating to the latest and greatest. That excellent advice about 'quality being remembered long after price is forgotten' certainly holds true here. While one brand of board may appear to have a cheaper purchase price, if they all have to be replaced throughout the school in five or six years because they have fallen so far behind a longer-lasting, slightly more expensive board, it will prove to be a false economy. Consider the total cost of ownership over the expected life of the technology.

Buy the best projectors the school can afford. If there is a weak link in today's IWB system, the projector is probably it. A good projector should be able to throw out enough light to project a clear, bright image in normal room lighting conditions. The light from all projectors will get less intense over time and the globes will eventually need replacing. If there are projectors in every classroom, the cumulative cost of replacing globes every year or two can be quite significant, with a typical projector globe costing around $500. This is often a 'hidden' cost that many schools neglect to prepare for.

One of the most important selection criteria will be the value for money of the package being offered. The total package should include the cost of the board, the software, projector, mounting arm, installation costs including speakers, cabling, power, wall-plates, amplifiers, signal boosters and even a desktop computer to drive the system (if that is the method the school has opted for). Find out what accessories are included such as voting systems, drawing slates and so on. Ask about what sort of savings can be expected for getting multiple classrooms installed at the same time. Find out what sort of support and training are included in the package. Will the company provide a trainer to help get the teachers up to speed quickly? How much support will they give, and what will they charge for further support if it is needed? Ask these questions before any money is handed over.

And when you do get the quote, negotiate. It is a competitive marketplace and all the major vendors would love to have you as a customer. Don't be shy about questioning the first price you get and go back to your supplier to ask how costs could be reduced further. They want your business, so push them for a great deal.

Then get on with it!

Why not just a data projector?

Some people will contend that an interactive whiteboard is a waste of money because by just using a data projector they can achieve 80 per cent of what the IWB offers without the cost.

At first, it seems like a logical argument until you start to think it through. There is no doubt that a data projector on its own can be a very valuable addition to a classroom. It can give access to a wide range of digital resources, be used to display web pages or slideshows to a class, show movies and photos, and so on. The projector certainly fulfils a significant part of the IWB magic. But the projector is also a significant part of the cost. By the time the room is cabled up properly, with the projector, the board, the speakers, the cabling, the power and the labour to do the installation, the actual IWB is a relatively small part of the overall cost. It seems silly to spend all the money on installing a projector, getting it cabled and mounted properly and including all the necessary peripherals, only to leave the board out of the picture.

The only way to justify a projector-only approach on a cost–benefit basis is when the projector is not mounted in a classroom and instead is set up on a table at the front of the room at the start of each lesson. It is not hard to see that a manually set up projector with no accessories or peripherals versus a fully installed projector with IWB, audio and neat cabling is hardly an apples-with-apples comparison. Added to that is the fact that if they had to set it up manually at the start of each lesson, most teachers would simply not bother with the projector at all.

This 'projector on its own is as good as having an IWB' style of thinking almost always comes from teachers who have already had a projector in their classroom for some time. Computing teachers are generally the worst offenders. Because they have had a projector in their classrooms for a while they cannot see what all the fuss is about. Of course, they are partially correct … you CAN do a great deal more if you have a projector in your classroom, and having a projector on its own is certainly much more cost-effective than a complete IWB installation. They overlook an important point, however. Until the IWB rose to popularity a few years ago, most classrooms did not have a projector, and there would be little likelihood that projectors on their own would appear in most general-purpose classrooms unless the IWB was acting as the driving force for getting them there. It is all very well to say that a projector on its own is just as good as an IWB, but the point is that without the IWB most classrooms will never get the projector.

But the real point they miss is that an IWB is designed to be a student-centric technology—or at least a student-and-teacher-centric technology. It is designed to get teachers and/or students working together to solve problems in full view of the class, focusing group attention on a shared board that all class members can see. The act of physically walking up to the board and actually pointing, touching and interacting with objects on the screen is entirely different to the act of wiggling a disembodied mouse cursor around on a screen that bears little direct link to the person doing the wiggling. Being seated at a computer and dragging things around on a large remote screen is an entirely different proposition to standing at the board and using your finger or a pen, pointing to the object you are talking about. It seems like a subtlety, but it is a major differentiator between the two ideas.

The other thing to consider is that an IWB encourages student participation by getting students to approach the board themselves and interact with it. In a projector-only classroom the technology is invariably driven by the teacher.

The bottom line is that while having a projector in your classroom is a wonderful thing, it is most definitely not the same thing as having an interactive whiteboard, no matter what anyone tries to tell you.

COMMITTING TO THE STRATEGY

In closing this chapter it is worth pondering an idea proposed many years ago by Sun Tzu in *The Art of War*, his highly influential book on ancient Chinese military warfare tactics: that it is usually not the strategy that counts so much as the commitment to the strategy. This ancient wisdom remains good advice as you ponder your choices for implementing interactive whiteboards in your school. Yes, it is important to do the homework and ensure that the choices are the best for the school, the students, the teachers and the budget. It is certainly worth talking to all the major IWB vendors, comparing their products, checking out the range of accessories and options. It is tempting to look at the new technologies on the horizon and consider delaying a decision until you see what is forthcoming; and it is scary to know whether you are buying the 'right' product or spending money on technology that could turn out to be a poor choice. However, it is easy to over-analyse things. The truth is that most of those things are probably far less important than you imagine. It is not about the strategy—it is about the commitment to the strategy. It is about making a decision to move forward with IWBs in your school and sticking to it. It is about supporting teachers with the right professional development and training. It is about school leadership stepping up to the challenge of making some significant cultural shifts in their school. It is about ensuring that the quality of teaching is sound and effective, so that technology can enhance it.

In other words, the choice of technology—hardboard versus softboard, Mac versus PC, laptops versus desktops, and so on—is not what will ultimately guarantee success for your IWB project, and nor will it doom you to failure. The choice of board for use throughout the school is nowhere near as important as getting all the human variables right. In fact, the choice of board for the school could well be one of the last decisions that need to be made.

The bottom line is that all of the known brands of IWBs are very good. None will let you down. There are schools that swear by their choice of every one of the major IWBs. The real task here is to think about the way in which the technology will be used to support quality teaching practices in your school. Get that part right and everything else becomes a relatively minor issue.

CHAPTER 4

E-TEACHING

For many people, the enormous change that has taken place in the last few decades has redefined the way they do their work. Many people work in jobs that did not exist a generation ago, performing tasks that would be unrecognised by their grandparents or even their parents. This rapid global change has had a major impact on many industries, often reshaping and redefining them, sometimes even causing them to disappear completely, unable to adapt with the speed and flexibility required for survival.

Paradoxically, the one area that seems to have so far resisted these changes the most is education—'paradoxically' because the stated goal of most education systems is to prepare our children for the future, and yet education systems as a whole have been woefully slow at identifying, acknowledging and adapting to the changes required to prepare for this future. Far too many classrooms are still little more than four walls, a teaching board and rows of tables and chairs; far too many teachers still believe the traditional tools for learning—textbooks, worksheets, the conventional teaching board—are enough; and in far too many classrooms the teaching tends to be a one-way experience, with the teacher at the front imparting knowledge to students who passively absorb these facts in order to repeat them back in an exam.

The problem for schools is that our students are not stuck in this same time warp. Outside of school they live in an always-on world of high-speed access to a global network—a world of instant communications and engaging multimedia. Armed with computers, mobile phones and social networks they have easy access to enormous quantities of information. They want information on demand. They need to multitask. They love to collaborate. For too many of our students, coming to school means 'powering down'.

The question, then, is how can our schools respond to these changes? How can our classrooms change to accommodate the needs of learners in the twenty-first century?

Thankfully, the last few years have seen a number of signs that things are slowly starting to change. More and more educators are using the Internet and Web 2.0 to form online communities, tapping into tools of connectivity to assist them in spreading the word about this need for change. This new connectedness of the online educational community is generating millions of conversations that are starting to have a grassroots impact on educational systems around the world, and the consequence is that these much-needed changes are becoming obvious to more and more educators.

Interactive whiteboards have the potential to play a major part in helping to shape this educational change. Their hybrid nature—that of being a cross between a computer and a traditional teaching board—means that of all the technologies that could be used in our schools, IWBs are potentially the most likely to bring about these changes to the greatest number of classrooms. Because they are capable of providing access to this new world of digital resources for the 'great unwashed masses' who are primarily teachers and not technologists, IWBs would seem to be the obvious tool for bringing relatively quick systemic change to a system that desperately needs it.

So it is time to explore the new world of 'e-teaching'.

Many of us have heard the term 'e-learning'. It usually describes the act of learning using technology and might be defined as 'the use of information and communication technologies to enhance the act of learning'. It often refers especially to remote or distance learning where teacher and student are physically separated from each other, but it is increasingly being used in a blended learning mode where some course content is delivered face to face and some is delivered via the e-learning system. Online learning platforms such as Moodle or Blackboard are typical of e-learning environments, which students log into in order to work through documents, tasks and activities to support a course of study, or which in some cases are actually the entire course of study. Students are also able to submit assignments electronically through the learning system, creating digital workflows between teacher and student.

If e-learning is all about learning using technology, then e-teaching ought to be a term used to describe the act of teaching using technology. A definition of e-teaching might be 'the use of information and communication technologies to enhance the act of teaching'.

Well-run classrooms have always been—and will always be—highly personal places and good teachers address this through a well-differentiated curriculum that caters to the individual learning needs of each student. There is no argument that great learning takes place when learners are able to learn at their own pace, engaging and interacting with ideas in ways that are personally meaningful. Writing, creating, designing, thinking, problem solving … these kinds of activities can be intensely personal and most learners will construct meaning for themselves in their own heads, in their own learning styles, as they work through these higher-order activities. That is essentially how real learning works.

Teaching is a little different. It is primarily a group activity. As teachers teach, they usually work with groups of learners and try to lead them on a path of discovery, exposing them to ideas and concepts that they may not yet have come into contact with. Teaching to a group is about unpacking and explaining concepts, encouraging discussion, challenging preconceptions and building knowledge. In a world where we focus a great deal on the value of learning, it is important not to lose sight of the value of teaching. Even teachers who believe passionately in the ideals of student-centred constructivist learning willingly acknowledge that there are still times when the most effective way to lead students from where they are to where they need to be is to explicitly teach them the things they need.

Which factor makes the biggest difference to effective learning? Recent research into this question has proven indisputably that the number one factor for successful learning is quality teaching. Not class size, not the school budget, not more standardised testing—but having a passionate teacher with outstanding knowledge of what he or she is teaching and letting them use that passion and knowledge to inspire their students to excel.

If excellence in teaching quality is the critical factor for student success, where does e-teaching fit in and how does e-teaching support this notion of quality teaching? The concept of e-teaching is fairly straightforward: infuse your lessons with rich media, digital resources and engaging communication technologies. What is perhaps not so obvious is that when we start to use technology and rich media on a routine basis in our classrooms, the pedagogy—or style of teaching—actually starts to change as well. The nature of teaching that takes place in a technology-rich environment starts to change, moving away from a 'content delivery' approach and more towards a deeper, more personal understanding of key concepts. And one of the very best ways to move a classroom—and therefore the teaching that takes place in that classroom—towards an engaging, media-rich environment is with the wise use of interactive whiteboards.

If you have ever taken your class to the computer room to work on a task, you know how engaged students can become when they use technology. If you are in the fortunate situation of having individual access to computers, either through a one-to-one program where every student has their own notebook computer or in a school where there are enough computers that students can gain access whenever they need them, you will no doubt have observed that technology makes a huge difference to student motivation and engagement. Kids like using computers. Unlike many traditional forms of classroom activity, it is not unusual to get to the end of a lesson using computers and the students just don't want to stop what they are doing. If the task is interesting enough and the technology is available enough, it is astounding to watch young people work with computers.

Simply having access to computers can go some way towards addressing the 'digital native' needs of our students; however, if we are to be effective educators—that is, quality teachers—then we need to tap into this rich motivation that technology brings, but in a way more suited to the group environment that the act of teaching is so often based around.

As teachers begin working with IWB technology in their classrooms and start thinking about this idea of e-teaching, they usually go through three fairly predictable phases, starting with basic IWB adaptations of things they have always done, through to presenting lessons in sophisticated, highly interactive ways. These phases may be summed up as follows:

- Phase 1: To start with, teachers persist in doing old things in old ways.
- Phase 2: As they start to understand the technology, teachers continue doing those old things, but in new ways.
- Phase 3: As they begin to master the technology, teachers gradually start trying new things in new ways.

Let us look at these phases in more detail.

PHASE 1: DOING OLD THINGS IN OLD WAYS

In this early phase, teachers may have the IWB technology in their classroom but it has not really changed anything yet. Although the interactive whiteboard is in the room, it is mainly used in exactly the same way as the old conventional whiteboard. In fact, many teachers in this phase will tell you that their old conventional whiteboard was much better (and for the sorts of things they are doing, they are probably right!).

Typical characteristics of this stage include:

- Notes and diagrams are still handwritten on the board as the lesson is taught.
- Lesson content consists primarily of Word documents or scanned text and diagrams.
- Limited use is made of the IWB's toolset.
- Lessons are not usually prepared in advance.
- Lessons do not take advantage of interactive features.
- Lessons are not saved at the end of class.
- The teacher works in isolation, not sharing resources with others.

This phase is painful for the teacher. The amount of effort required to use an IWB in this manner far outweighs the potential benefits. The nuisance factor of having to connect a computer, start a projector, deal with an unfamiliar and cluttered environment, all to do exactly the same sorts of things that were being done with a regular whiteboard with considerably less effort and expense, makes it all seem like an outrageously silly arrangement. If they do spend time in this phase, most teachers usually get past it fairly quickly, simply because the pain of staying there is too great. They can either continue to work like this and to complain about the infernal technology and how pointless it is, or they can move on to the next phase where it starts to make a little more sense.

PHASE 2: DOING OLD THINGS, BUT IN NEW WAYS

In this phase, teachers start to wise up about having an interactive whiteboard in the classroom. They are starting to feel that there has to be more to having an IWB than they are getting out of it right now. Maybe it comes from greater experience with the software or perhaps they have started to observe innovative IWB teaching from their colleagues, but as teachers move into this phase they start discovering that they can still use all their tried-and-true lesson ideas but just adapt them slightly to take advantage of the IWB's strengths. What they generally discover along the way is that teaching with an IWB requires a slightly different approach but it can get markedly different results.

Typical characteristics of this second phase include:

- Modification of existing paper-based worksheets and activities to work on the IWB.
- Greater use of flipchart-style lessons prepared in advance.
- Greater use of dragable, layered objects that can be moved around the screen, revealing existing words and objects.
- Greater reliance on resources found in the gallery or on the web.
- Effective use of software that works well on an IWB.
- All lessons saved for future use and reused.
- Lessons shared with other teachers to reduce individual workloads.
- Noticeably increased levels of student engagement and interest.

The motto for this phase should be 'working smarter, not harder'. Suddenly the IWB does not seem like such a nuisance any more and the payoffs for using it are making more sense. Because the lessons are starting to take advantage of greater levels of interactivity, students seem to be more engaged and interested in the work. Although individual lessons may take a little more time to prepare, the fact that they can be reused with multiple classes means that there are longer-term benefits, not to mention that the lesson preparation workload is able to be divided between teachers who share what they create.

PHASE 3: DOING NEW THINGS IN NEW WAYS

This is where it starts to get interesting. The penny finally drops about how powerfully interactive whiteboards can change the learning, and teachers start to truly reinvent the way they approach their lessons. As teachers spend more time with their IWB, they start to come up with completely new ways to convey course concepts to their students, often using much richer media such as video, audio, animation and interactivity.

This phase builds on the previous ones but is mainly characterised by lessons that are not mere digital versions of what could be done in the old ways. They are marked by creative teaching and innovative techniques that start to see teaching and learning move from mere content delivery to a far more meaningful exploration of lesson content through interactivity, rich media and greater student involvement. Because of this, attempting to identify 'typical' characteristics is not as straightforward as the first two phases, but it may include such things as:

- The use of short snippets of video or animation that do a far better job of explaining how something works rather than just simple diagrams.
- The inclusion of high-resolution photo images that give the ability to zoom in to inspect the finer details of an image.
- Tapping into the enormous libraries of interactive learning objects and embedding these in lessons so that students are able to easily explore the 'what if' possibilities.
- Greater use of software that enables students to manipulate ideas, seeing what happens to the final outcome if a variable is changed here or there.
- The ability to perform impractical or dangerous experiments via simulation that would never have been possible in a classroom or laboratory situation.
- The ability to engage with virtual worlds and simulated environments to explore possibilities that cannot be explored any other way.
- Increased levels of interactivity and student involvement, often raising questions that were unexpected but with answers that offer greater insight into and deeper understanding of a topic.
- The use of real-time video communication software to facilitate class-to-class collaboration, or even to bring in guest speakers over the web, so that students can ask questions and interact with others outside their classroom.
- The use of classroom interactive voting systems to gauge student understanding of key concepts in real time.

One of the things that become apparent as teachers move into this phase is that the associated skills needed to function effectively at this level move beyond just the use of the interactive whiteboard. As new approaches to teaching become apparent because of access to the IWB, so does the need grow to build related technology skills such as working with digital images, effectively searching the web, manipulating audio and video, discovering new software applications and so on. This is where IWBs seem to have the strongest Trojan horse effect, as the use of technology starts to become an embedded part of the teacher's repertoire for presenting lessons. Although on the surface the IWB is just the means of presenting lessons to the class, it is in fact acting as the catalyst for a far more embedded use of technology in the classroom generally.

Teachers who have spent time working with interactive technology often talk about how it has fundamentally changed their approach to teaching. This is a key aspect of the whole IWB debate, as it supports the assertion that we are not just adding yet another form of technology to the classroom, but rather having it become a truly transformative technology that potentially redefines the underlying pedagogy and improves the quality of the teaching and learning that takes place in those classrooms.

Following are comments from a few teachers about how IWBs have affected their work. These comments were collected from real teachers (via a short request using Twitter, an online personal networking tool) in response to the following question: *In what ways has an IWB affected your classroom and how you teach?*

Originally from the UK and now living in New Zealand, Simon Evans (http://educatingthedragon.edublogs.org) works as a consultant with Breathe Technology, a leading ICT professional development company in New Zealand. Until recently, Simon taught Year 3 at Peterhead School in Flaxmere where he used an Interwrite interactive whiteboard with his students.

> *The introduction of the interactive whiteboard into my classroom has really made a huge difference to how I teach. First of all, I began by simply using it just like you would an overhead projector. So I did a little bit of that, and as my knowledge of IWB technology grew, I was introduced to ways and means of incorporating it into my lessons, integrating it more fully. I then progressed into getting children interacting with it a little bit more. My students were able to access a wider variety of information, and I use it now for them to be able to drive their own learning. With the training provided by the IWB supplier broadening to include things like Skype and blogs and wikis it motivated me to find out more about the edublogosphere.*

Simon's comments are a good example of the three e-teaching phases that come from having regular access to an IWB. As you read his comment, notice the board was used initially as nothing more than a projector screen (doing old things in old ways), then moving on to more comprehensive uses with greater levels of student involvement (doing old things in new ways), leading finally to the discovery of completely new collaborative and web-based tools for learning (doing new things in new ways), opening up whole new avenues for learning in his classroom. Also interesting is that he describes the IWB as having made 'a huge difference to how I teach', further supporting the assertion that this is really all about pedagogy, not technology.

Australian teacher Jess McCulloch (http://www.technolote.com) teaches Chinese language to students at Hawkesdale P–12 College in country Victoria, and has been using a SMART Board in her classes for well over a year.

> The two biggest advantages of teaching with an IWB are increased student engagement (because the students are all dying to get their hands on the board and are eager to watch anything that's happening on it) and the ability to cater more effectively for kinaesthetic learners. Aspects of using an IWB such as the ability to show anything that's on your computer to the whole class easily and add notes to whatever it is you or the students are demonstrating, as well as being able to save students' work and class notes straight away and use them for other classes are fantastic advantages, but I think they are secondary to engagement and the ability to cater for different learning styles.

Saving class work for later review, catering for different learning styles and experiencing elevated levels of student engagement are not limited to technology-enabled classrooms; they are hallmarks of good teaching practice in the most general sense. But that is the point. The introduction of interactive whiteboards should be about teaching, not technology. Good teaching is good teaching. It always has been and always will be, and no technology should ever be a replacement for that. What IWBs can do, however, is to turbo-charge this teaching process through the simple introduction of accessible multimedia, on-demand web access and increased interactivity to make good teaching even better teaching.

As Jess goes on to say:

> The IWB is not the be-all and end-all to integrating technology into the classroom, and it is not necessarily an essential tool to have. But for a place to present to a class and for a tool to engage students by encouraging the hands-on aspect that so many students find important to their learning, it is a fantastic resource.

Cathy Nelson (http://blog.cathyjonelson.com) is the library media specialist at Conway Middle School, part of the Horry County School District in South Carolina in the US. She has worked with interactive whiteboards for a number of years, and has this to say about her dealings with IWBs:

Using the board, the slate and the Activotes seems to make my students much more excited. Everyone wants to touch the board, the slate, or hold the 'eggs'. Kids will come in asking what will we be doing that day, and then be mildly disappointed if they were not using the tools. Before, they NEVER asked.

Student engagement with the technology is a common theme that comes to the surface very quickly when you talk to any teacher who uses an IWB regularly. Young people love lessons where the IWB is used to make them more interesting.

Cathy goes on to say:

Some teachers want to use it just like an overhead projector, or worse, a worksheet. Nothing takes the life out of a student faster than a very dull worksheet. You have to be careful not to make lessons that could have just as easily been done as a worksheet.

This comment about not making IWB lessons that are simply a digital rehash of existing lessons is one of the keys to understanding the differences offered by an e-teaching approach. We don't need to use technology tools to do old things in old ways, or even to do old things in new ways. Where we get the most leverage from these tools is when we make the mental leap into phase 3 and begin to do new things in new ways—things that were largely impossible without the richly embedded, immersive use of technology across the curriculum that IWBs are really good at enabling.

Jess McCulloch reiterates this same point when she says:

Even though I know there is a lot more I can do with the IWB in my classroom, and I am trying to find more innovative ways to use it, I see other teachers who simply don't understand the potential of it. On several occasions I've been asked to swap out of my room so that another teacher can show a DVD to their class ... While an IWB is undoubtedly a fantastic screen for watching movies and DVDs on, to not explore its potential any further than that is wasting an incredible resource.

Again, most interesting are the different approaches to the use of the IWB by teachers who are clearly at different points of the adoption curve. There is nothing wrong with using an IWB screen to show a DVD to the class; in fact, because a fully installed IWB generally has a ceiling-mounted projector and wall-mounted speakers, they actually make excellent projection screens for showing DVDs. But the point is that to use them for something as mundane as showing a movie is missing out on the real benefits that they offer. For the enthusiastic IWB-using teacher, it can be somewhat frustrating to watch an IWB being used in this way by colleagues but it is part of the reality of allowing every teacher to make their way through the three phases.

In a recent UK study by Glover and Miller called *Missioners, Tentatives and Luddites* (2001), they identified three basic categories of teachers that happen to map nicely against these three phases. The 'Missioners' are those teachers who really get it. They have been to some training, they have regular access to an IWB in their classroom and they are starting to fly with it. Their teaching style is evolving to suit the new technology and they are starting to see the myriad of possibilities for doing new things in new ways. In many schools, these are the teachers on a mission to spread the word about how amazing they find the IWB. The 'Tentatives' are willing to give it a go, but are still just getting their head around the whole IWB concept. They use the boards, they see some advantages and they are learning all the time. They are not the IWB evangelists just yet, but they are positive and willing to play the game. These are often the teachers who are still doing the old things but in new ways, and they probably form the bulk of teaching staff at the moment. With some more training, a bit of hand holding and the right support, it is only a matter of time before these teachers are coming up with their own new and creative ways of using IWBs to help students learn better. The 'Luddites' still don't quite get it. For the most part they persist in teaching the same way they always did and see the IWB for its inconvenience rather than its potential. They do not yet fully appreciate that if they would only just rethink some of their approaches to teaching to take advantage of the IWBs strengths, things could change very quickly. They continue to use the IWB in the the same way they use a regular whiteboard, if indeed they use it at all, and then wonder why it does not make a noticeable difference to student learning.

It has been said that a useful definition of insanity is to continue to do the same things yet expect different results. As you talk to teachers who use their IWBs well, the same common theme keeps coming to the surface: good teaching with an IWB means rethinking the way you teach.

CLASSROOM AGILITY—TEACHING 'ON THE FLY'

There is another important aspect of e-teaching worth mentioning. It is all about having a classroom that is agile enough to change the course of a lesson at short notice to pursue unplanned-for student interests.

This is almost impossible to do well in a conventional classroom, but the teacher's ability to instantly divert the direction of a lesson according to student interests or questions, and then back it up with immediate access to information and answers, has enormous benefits. Having on-demand access to resources like the World Wide Web and being able to share search results with the whole class on a single big screen is an extremely powerful teaching and learning tool. Learning is often about connecting ideas, where talking about one concept will raise further questions. In a conventional classroom, a student who asks a good question about the topic being discussed in class often only gets that question dealt with in a fairly superficial way. Even if the teacher did have time to divert the lesson to answer the question, chances are that the resources needed to fully explore the answer would not be immediately at hand. If the answer is not in the textbook, the temptation is to gloss over it. If the teacher does have the answer, the students normally have to just listen to the explanation, unaided by visuals or media resources because the teacher was unable to plan for the unexpected question in advance.

In most cases the standard answer given to the student is something like: 'Great question. Why don't you find that out tonight for homework and tell us tomorrow?' So now, not only does the class fail to get the benefit of a potentially good discussion arising from the question, but the keen student who asked it now has an extra piece of homework to do. No wonder kids stop asking questions!

A better response would be: 'Great question! Let's find out together right now!' Wouldn't it be so much better if these diversion points, these great questions that arise in class, could be dealt with as a group? Surely the rest of the class would also benefit from finding out the answers. For students, talking and discussing and discovering together are an engaging interactive process in itself, especially when the question comes directly from one of their peers. They also get to see the information literacy process in action, modelled for them on the big screen by the teacher if needed.

Amanda Signal (http://ruthere.edublogs.org), a primary teacher from Auckland, New Zealand, makes the point about the IWB's agility:

*Having an IWB gives you the freedom to follow where kids take the lesson.
Instead of having to 'come back to that later' because you haven't got
resources or items to more fully dive into those ideas, you can utilise the
Internet or multimedia or other resources to delve into the kids' ideas then
and there and be able to look into them more closely. The kids don't just
get to see images; they can manipulate things such as with Google Earth
when exploring the world, or move pieces of text to make up stories. With
an IWB, students can have a lot more ownership over lessons and the
direction they take.*

Now that's real interactivity!

AIMING FOR AMBIGUITY

Interactive whiteboards are called 'interactive' because they encourage
students to interact with the lesson. But the notion of interactivity is
usually limited to the idea of physical interactivity—students getting up
from their seat, coming to the board and physically touching the surface
of the board to fulfil some task.

In his excellent book, *Interactive Whiteboards: A practical guide for primary
teachers* (2008), Australian IWB expert Peter Kent talks about a concept he
calls 'ambiguity'. Kent uses the term to refer to learning situations that
are specifically designed to create an intellectual juxtaposition of one idea
against another and how by setting up apparently opposing or alternative
ways of viewing information, students are forced to see that information
differently. Consequently, when information is ambiguous and open-
ended it creates a fertile environment for rich discussion and can provoke
students to see a problem from multiple viewpoints, often prompting
them to debate and argue for their viewpoint to be heard.

Getting students to argue their case, to explain and express their
point of view and defend it to their classmates, is a far more useful form
of interactivity than the 'getting a student to come to the board and drag
a box around' sort of interactivity that we so often think of when we talk
about IWBs. Getting intellectual interactivity is a far more desirable goal
than simply getting physical interactivity.

IWBs can be very good at enabling teachers to prompt and provoke
students with jarring ideas that cause them to think deeply about an
idea. They can be used to effectively create hypothetical scenarios in
which there are no clear right or wrong answers, and students are

forced to defend their values, justify their choices, explain their reasoning or propose their solution.

So try not to just use the IWB to create activities that require students to drag a text label around to match up with an unlabelled object. It is a good starting point, but this sort of activity is a relatively low-level thinking task that requires minimal real intellectual engagement from students. Except perhaps for very young children who are still learning to recognise words and associate them with pictures, most older students are capable of so much more. Getting a student to physically interact with the board is good, but it only engages that one student at a time. A well-designed learning activity, filled with ambiguous ideas that challenge every student to intellectually engage with the bigger ideas behind the lesson, should be the goal of every teacher as they move towards mastering their IWBs. Work on getting students' minds to interact, not just their hands!

BUT WHAT DOES THE RESEARCH SAY?

It is all very well and good for individual teachers to talk about the benefits that come from using an interactive whiteboard. But what about the research? What does it say about the effectiveness of IWBs?

There have been a number of studies over the past few years into just how effective interactive technology might be in a classroom. On the whole, it is overwhelmingly positive. Independent research (Balanskat, Blamire & Kefala, 2006) has shown that, when used wisely, IWBs can produce a significant improvement to student learning. 'Used wisely' is the key phrase. As teachers make the move towards e-teaching through the implementation of IWB technology, they should bear in mind that IWBs do need to be 'used wisely', and this primarily means ensuring that the pedagogy underlying the technology is implemented soundly. It is pointless to expect any sort of gains to be made unless the teaching style taps into the potential of the board so that this e-teaching ideal is given a chance to flourish.

Much of the existing research has come from the UK, where interactive whiteboards have already made massive inroads into classrooms—more than 60 per cent of all UK classrooms are fitted with an IWB. This extensive penetration of IWBs into schools has given the UK literature a critical mass of users from which to draw some sound conclusions.

Higgins et al. (2005) note that for the use of IWBs to be justified they must be used to take learning above and beyond that which was possible with conventional whiteboards, or even other kinds of projection technology (that is, a move towards new things in new ways). Teachers in the UK taking part in the interactive whiteboard pilot project were extremely positive about the technology and were convinced that improvements in teaching and learning were among the changes brought about by use of IWBs. In their study, Higgins et al. found that IWBs made a difference to several aspects of classroom interaction. They noted that there tended to be a faster pace (measured by the number of interactions between teachers and students) in the whiteboard lessons compared with the non-whiteboard lessons.

With regard to pedagogy, Higgins et al.'s research also found an embedding effect whereby even a year later teachers who had adopted the IWB as a core part of their teaching toolkit continued to ask better and more open questions, probing students for further information or more detailed explanations—all characteristics of quality teaching techniques. They also found that teachers gave richer, more evaluative responses during whiteboard lessons and addressed follow-up questions to the whole class rather than to an individual student.

The *ERNIST ICT school portraits* (2004) clearly demonstrate that there is a positive effect of IWBs on teaching and learning, even when they are used only to support existing practice. However, this study found that IWBs were often the catalyst for teachers to replace existing practice with more interactive, constructivist approaches. Contributors to this study noted that the interactive technology tended to help teachers become even more innovative in the resources they were able to bring to students, and that students appeared to learn more effectively when presented with the wide range of stimuli that IWBs were able to bring before them. It was also noted that the boards in no way stifled teaching; in fact, the IWB software was seen to be so flexible and easy to use that most, if not all, teachers were able to use them regularly with few problems.

In another study by Miller, Glover and Averis (2004) it was noted that teachers tended to use IWBs in one of three ways: either to support an existing didactic approach (another way of saying old things in old ways); an interactive approach (old things in new ways); or what they referred to as an 'enhanced interactive approach' (new things in new ways). This last approach was found to exploit the interactive capabilities of the technology in a way that most successfully integrated with the conceptual and cognitive development of students.

In plain English, teachers who really used the boards well, in ways that were innovative, engaging and beyond the realm of what could be done with conventional classroom tools, had students that learned more effectively.

As an interesting aside, in two different studies into the effects of IWBs on teachers—Higgins et al. (2005) and Underwood et al. (2006)—found that the overwhelming majority of teachers participating in the interactive whiteboard project in the UK (that is, some 98 per cent) said that they became more confident in using ICT in general as a direct result of using an IWB. There is the validation for the Trojan horse theory right there!

Incidentally, apart from having an IWB, the other key factor uncovered by the studies was that if one truly wanted to assist teachers to develop general ICT skills, they needed to have their own laptop computer. It ought to come as no surprise that if every teacher is given their own computer, an IWB and enough professional development, training and support to ensure that this all gets used wisely, then the benefits begin to follow. (It is critical to have the training and support part, though—the hardware on its own is not enough.)

Finally, some great insights from Miller, Glover and Averis (2005), whose research team from Keele University worked with twelve partner-school mathematics departments to evaluate the effectiveness of teaching when IWB technology is used to advantage:

> Evidence suggests that the presentational advantages of IWB use are considerable and that the consequent motivational gain is to be welcomed. However, it is also clear that neither of these add to teaching effectiveness unless they are supported by teachers who understand the nature of interactivity as a teaching and learning process and who integrate the technology to ensure lessons that are both cohesive and conceptually stimulating.

See? It is not about the hardware.

The final summation of e-teaching can go to Brette Lockyer, an Australian teacher who responded via Twitter to the question of how IWBs have changed her teaching:

> When I plan an IWB activity or do it, I ask: 'Is this the better way?' Now I am asking that question for all activities. Good feeling! Having an IWB in my room has made me question everything I do now.

Thanks, Brette. We couldn't have said it better.

CHAPTER **5**

EIGHT KEY PRINCIPLES FOR EFFECTIVE IWB TEACHING

Now that you have an interactive whiteboard in your classroom, what comes next? Hopefully you are enthusiastically pondering all the wonderful possibilities that lie ahead. Maybe you are re-evaluating the way you teach and the way you approach learning in your classroom. You may be mentally redesigning your assessment procedures, rethinking your classroom organisation or busily bookmarking as many engaging, interactive web resources as you can find. Or maybe you are not so excited. Maybe your IWB has been thrust upon you by a school policy that you are still not quite sure you agree with and you are feeling a little intimidated or nervous about the idea of using this strange new tool in your classroom.

Wherever you find yourself in the big scheme of things, there are a few basic principles to bear in mind as you embark upon your adventure of teaching with an IWB. Following are eight important ideas that will help make the adventure even more rewarding for you and your students.

1 BE PROFICIENT

There is an often-quoted statistic regarding Microsoft Word that contends most users only ever use 10 per cent of the capability of that program. While you could probably quibble over the actual percentage or debate how the 10 per cent figure was arrived at, it would be hard to dispute the general principle that most people never really discover the full functionality of Microsoft's Office software and relatively few users get far beyond the ability to type some text, change its font and maybe stick in some clip art, without ever realising how many clever features exist in Word. In many places, anyone who can do even marginally more is seen as the geeky expert.

And so, when it comes to software we tend to have a degree of acceptance mentality that it is ok to be a user who knows just enough 'to get by' and that anyone who rises beyond the basic levels of use is some sort of 'super-geek'. When it comes to using IWBs and their associated software, however, there are some compelling reasons to break out of this mindset and decide that becoming a proficient user of your IWB's software is worth doing.

Regardless of the brand of IWB your school uses, there is probably a significant overlap in the tools and features across the different brands. All will usually have the ability to draw basic shapes, add lines and write text. All will usually have a 'window shade' feature, a gallery of objects and the ability to drag objects around the screen. In the competitive IWB marketplace most of the commonly used features are quickly becoming part of a standard set of IWB tools regardless of the brand of board you use, and this is a good thing. It means that teachers moving from one board to another will generally be able to find their way around, or at least will take the time to find the tool they need if they know it is likely to be 'in there somewhere'. Once you understand the basic principles for using 'your' brand of IWB, the learning curve between different brands is surprisingly easy.

However, there is a great deal to be said for taking the time to become really proficient with the software for the brand of board you use most often. Knowing what tools you have available to you (and where to find them) leads to a much greater sense of mastery with your IWB, making you much more likely to use the technology in creative and spontaneous ways. Something as simple as knowing what diagrams and interactive tools you have at your disposal in the gallery can do wonders for your confidence levels; whether it may be knowing how to quickly grab some interactive dice in the middle of a maths lesson, how to easily insert a short video clip from YouTube to show a science principle, or how to use the camera tool to screengrab and annotate over a web page in an English lesson—the ability to effectively use the tools of your IWB environment cannot be emphasised enough.

Of course, having said that, you should not expect to be an expert immediately. For many teachers, just starting out with an IWB, simply having the ability to project large-scale interactive text and then scribble over it with a virtual pen, is a major step forward in their use of technology and the importance of this should not be overlooked. Never mind all the potential that comes from integrating sound and video into your lessons, tapping into pre-made learning objects, using screen captures, or window shading, or infinitely cloned objects … if you are just starting out with an IWB it is still ok to be excited by the new things that it lets you do, regardless of how simple they may be to the grizzled old experts that have been using IWBs for a much longer time.

It is quite normal to be dazzled by all the 'cool stuff' you can do, but eventually you start to realise that if this new toy is going to have a permanent place in your classroom, then you should probably start to get to know it as well as you can. While an IWB is a pretty fancy piece of hardware, the real magic—as we pointed out earlier—is what one learns to do with the software. The more intimately you know your software, the more confident, competent and creative you will feel about the whole IWB experience. This leads to more interesting lessons and a general feeling that the IWB truly is a tool for better learning and teaching.

One of the really interesting things about IWBs is the way they get you using more of your computer's potential to act as a digital hub. Remember, the board itself is a fairly benign technology—it is really just a large touch screen for driving your computer—and yet an increased confidence in the use of the IWB seems to help teachers unlock the digital potential of their computers in ways that they would never have done if it relied on just using the computer on its own. This is perhaps yet another example of the 'Trojan horse' effect that IWBs are having in the creation of digital learning environments.

The bottom line is to get to know your IWB. Explore the software that comes with your board. Spend time looking through the menus. Click on the toolbar icons to see what they do. Set aside some time to just play with the software. Do this exploring with other teachers if possible. Share your discoveries. Brainstorm ideas for making use of the features you find. Watch others teach with IWBs and ask them how they did things that you may not have seen before. Listen to podcasts or read blogs about the use of IWBs.

This is your new reality. It will be so much more fun if you are good at it.

2 BE ORGANISED

Being organised with your IWB refers to the physical issues such as the type of board you use, where it is placed, how it is set up and how the computer that drives it is configured. It also encompasses the software you use and the preparation you put into developing your digital teaching resources. The more organised you are with all of this, the more able you will be to walk into your classroom and teach, making the IWB just another seamless tool in your classroom.

So what does being organised mean? It means:

- having a board mounted in your classroom in a central position where the whole class can see and access it;
- having the board wired to power, sound and the web so that all of these things can be accessed without having to do any technical wizardry with wires;
- creating a digital hub situation where the board can be used to manage, control and access a wide range of digital resources such as the Internet, network file shares and online learning objects;
- having on-demand access to peripheral devices, whether they are fairly basic ones like scanners and printers, or slightly more exotic ones like graphics tablets, GPS units and data probes. What you have connected to your digital hub will depend on what you want to do in your classroom, but the key point is that if you plan to use these digital resources as part of your teaching, and you plan to use the IWB as the primary means of sharing these tools with the class, then it is important that these things are connected and work properly. This means having them correctly installed, having the correct drivers and, if necessary, having the appropriate network permissions to run them properly. Some peripheral devices are notoriously troublesome, so check that everything works as you expect it to. The middle of a lesson is a bad time to discover that some rogue driver software will not play along with your planned activity!

Of course, the truth is that the IWB is just a way to drive your computer in a more classroom-friendly manner, so the effectiveness of what you do with your IWB will, to some extent, be dependent on the effectiveness of what you can do with your computer. And this raises another issue about the way you might choose to set up your IWB: will you drive it with a desktop computer that lives in your classroom and is permanently connected to the board, or will you drive it with a laptop computer that you plug in when required? Both options have advantages and disadvantages, and your choice will be influenced by several factors including whether it is a primary school or high school setting. Desktop computers permanently connected to the boards are generally well suited to primary classrooms, while portable laptops may work better in a secondary setting as teachers move around from room to room.

Obviously, this latter approach requires every teacher to carry their own laptop computer, and for some schools this BYO-laptop strategy is not appropriate. The other problem with having laptop computers that move from room to room is that they require the constant connection of the laptop to an IWB. This is usually fairly simple—it just requires plugging the IWB into the laptop's video output and connecting the IWB to the computer—but it also may involve recalibrating the board before every lesson. None of this is very difficult or time consuming, but it is still an extra couple of steps to consider. On the other hand, the advantage of the BYO-laptop approach is that teachers have full-time access to their own computers, making it easier to prepare resources at school or at home. For many teachers, being able to take their own computer home and prepare lessons in advance then just plug in to the IWB in the classroom is a big advantage.

The alternative, in-class desktop computer approach requires having the lesson resources prepared in advance and storing them on the school network so they can be accessed in the classroom. Working between school and home then requires work to be emailed back and forth or carried on memory sticks—not an overly difficult prospect, but just something else to consider in deciding which method you will use for driving your classroom IWBs.

3 BE INTERACTIVE

Not everyone loves IWBs. In fact, one of the main arguments against them goes something like this … For many years the traditional classroom has been a place where the teacher stands in front of the students and lectures them about content that they need to know. This is generally considered a bad thing, as it places the teacher and not the students at the centre of the learning process. Reacting against this traditional model, innovative teachers have worked hard to build a classroom environment where the students are the focus of learning, where curiosity is more valued than content, where education is not just about remembering things the teacher tells students but rather about interacting with ideas in ways that make personal sense to them. This notion of constructivist learning is at the heart of a twenty-first century approach to learning. Then along come these newfangled interactive whiteboards and suddenly we are putting the teacher back on the stage in front of the students, and we begin to wonder where our constructivist classrooms went!

It is true that if all teachers do with an IWB is to replace their regular chalkboard with something a bit fancier and a lot more expensive, then they are missing the whole point. Although the two technologies may look similar (they both appear to be a teaching board mounted on the front wall of the classroom), it would be a huge mistake to think that an IWB is simply a more modern version of a chalkboard. Unlike the chalkboard, the IWB is not a tool for the teacher; it is a resource to be used by the whole class.

There are important pedagogical issues surrounding how teachers prepare lessons using the available software and how they use the interactive features of the IWB to deliver concepts in ways that can be dramatically more effective. If they just use the IWB to do what they have always done on their regular whiteboard, they are wasting their time and money. It is probably more time consuming and troublesome to use an IWB in this way, and in all likelihood will be far less effective as a teaching tool. There are still many teachers who have not yet come to terms with the idea that the IWB is not just a replacement for a traditional whiteboard and who still start each lesson with a blank flipchart or notebook page, creating notes on it during the lesson in exactly the same way they would have done on a traditional whiteboard (and some don't even save it at the end of the lesson!).

The defining feature of an interactive whiteboard is interactivity. If you don't learn to tap into the interactive aspect of IWB technology, you may as well not use one.

So what do we mean by interactivity? Interactivity simply means that your IWB resources should be designed in such a way that students can interact with them, either physically or mentally. Interactivity for a Year 1 class could be as simple as taking turns at coming up to the board during storytime and dragging characters around the board to help describe the story, pressing a picture of a cow to hear a 'moo' sound, or making a cartoon frog hop along a number line as they learn to add. As we move into secondary school, interactivity could still be about students coming up to the board and physically interacting with it, but it could be equally interactive in the mental sense when the teacher uses a piece of software like GeoGebra to draw a parabolic equation on the board and then manipulates it around the Cartesian grid to show students how the equation changes to reflect the new position. Interactivity could mean using software like Google Earth to pick up the globe, rotate it and zoom in, showing animated layers to demonstrate some geographical principle, or manipulating objects in a virtual physics environment like Phun, or using a learning object to demonstrate a heart pumping blood through the arteries.

The interactive nature of the board will mean different things to different teachers in different classrooms, teaching different subjects with different age groups, but the important thing is to use digital resources in a way that allows students to engage, interact and manipulate the key ideas and concepts, even if they are not always out of their seats actually touching the board—although there is certainly nothing wrong with that!

So build your lessons with interactivity in mind. Go right back to basics and think about the principles you are trying to get across to your students. Ask yourself, what is the important idea that the students must take away from this lesson? Then use the digital environment of interactivity to build lessons that engage and stimulate their minds, whether by including audio or video resources, making objects movable or dragable, or enabling objects to be flexibly manipulated in ways that show their inherent qualities. Think about how you might get the students to interact with the content, challenging them mentally and getting them to explore ideas in a way that prods their mind and provokes them into understanding at a deeper level.

4 BE FLEXIBLE

Most teachers are fairly organised. Many plan their lessons well in advance and create useful resources and activities for their students, which they hope will be relevant and engaging. They walk into their classrooms fully prepared, ready to impart all their wonderful knowledge to their eagerly awaiting students.

The problem is that learning in the twenty-first century no longer really works like that. The act of teaching is no longer just about simply imparting a predefined body of knowledge to passive students. It is about helping students to learn and explore ideas—and sometimes what they need to learn is not exactly what you planned to teach them. So being a teacher in the twenty-first century sometimes involves flexibility and a willingness to take the occasional detour into areas that you had not planned for.

One of the really great things about having an IWB permanently set up in your classroom is the ability to easily take these detours into areas that were not part of your original lesson plan. Sometimes, the most valuable learning that takes place in a lesson comes from these detours and not from the actual lesson. In fact, the more you teach with an IWB and the more proficient you become with their use, the more flexibly and fluidly you will find yourself able to move from your planned lesson, head down into an interesting detour, explore it, and then smoothly pick up into the planned lesson again.

Flexibility is a valuable quality in a classroom, just as it is in other areas of life. Think about your last holiday trip. You probably planned where to go, pre-booked your accommodation, bought the maps and worked out which roads to take. But then, as you set out for your holiday, you found that the traffic was a little heavier than you expected and caused you to take a different route, or you discovered a delightful little café for lunch that you did not know existed, or the weather was not what you thought it would be and that trip to the theme park had to be postponed, or the car broke down and you had to call for a tow … There could be many reasons why you would need to make adjustments to your original plans, and the interesting thing is that sometimes it is these side trips and detours that end up being the most fun, most interesting, and often the most memorable parts of the holiday.

The learning (and teaching) that takes place in a classroom is no different. Students often ask great questions or make insightful comments during your carefully planned lessons, and these deserve to be explored. Just like the holiday detour, following the occasional diversion that arises from an unexpected in-class question can also be the most interesting and valuable parts of a lesson—and the most fun. One very depressing situation in our classrooms is when students have a genuine interest or curiosity to learn about something, but the teacher cannot stop and take the time to explore or explain it because they are so busy 'getting through' the other stuff. If we accept that real learning takes place when students are genuinely engaged and interested in an idea, then we really need to make the time to do a little unplanned exploring with them every now and then.

An IWB that is permanently mounted in your classroom, permanently connected to the Internet (or a range of other worthwhile software applications) and able to be used by a teacher who is confident and comfortable in its operation, is a powerful tool for making these diversions from the original intent of the lesson plan. The ability to flexibly divert a lesson 'on the fly' in order to check on a relevant website or digital resource, to quickly find associated information or supporting data, to access relevant video or photographic images, and then smoothly move back into the flow of the original lesson can do wonders for satisfying the curiosity of your students.

Done well, this sort of flexibility can create an extremely powerful, engaging and motivating learning environment that is simply not possible to achieve without the large-screen digital-hub environment created with an IWB.

5 BE CONSTRUCTIVE

Imagine trying to learn to play golf without ever swinging a golf club, or learning to play the guitar without actually picking up the instrument. What about learning to cook, or do karate, or speak Mandarin with only the help of a handbook?

Knowing the theory of how to do things is not usually enough. It would be hard to learn any of these things without actually *doing* it. Having someone simply tell us how to swing the golf club or play the guitar, while possibly helpful, would be no real substitute for doing it ourselves. A whole learning theory exists to support this idea. Called 'constructivism', its proponents include people like Dewey, Piaget, Vygotsky and Papert. Constructivist learning theory suggests that if we really want to learn something so that we understand it, then we need to somehow engage with it, manipulate it, touch it, move it and play with it. It is through this process of play, exploration and manipulation that our understanding of the thing we are trying to learn about is constructed.

So how does this relate to having an interactive whiteboard in your classroom? One of the very important aspects of IWB lesson design is to create lessons that enable your students to learn through playing with ideas. Unlike a traditional teaching board, IWBs support the creation of objects that can be dragged and moved by students. They support the on-screen manipulation of data to show 'what if' scenarios and hypothetical situations. They enable multiple sensory inputs in multimedia forms like text, images, audio, video and animation. They allow the hyperlinking of resources so that objects can become clickable and therefore be explored. Even in a typical high school situation where lessons can still be somewhat teacher-centred in the sense that the teacher often drives the board, this highly interactive digital environment goes a long way to providing an explorative, manipulative environment that promotes constructivist-type learning experiences.

It is tempting to want to play teacher and maintain the dominant role in the classroom. But teachers need to learn to step aside and allow the students to take over. Let the students drive the IWB. Let them suggest ways it could be used. Learn to let go and hand the board over to your students. And then, learn to let go and hand the whole lesson over to your students when it is appropriate. You might be amazed at just how engaged in the learning process the students can be if only we will allow them to be.

6 BE OPEN-MINDED

Teachers who seem to get the most out of having an interactive whiteboard tend to be creative and open-minded to new ideas. Their colleagues sometimes see them as having some sort of 'super-geek' status because they appear to be able to learn to use technology more easily than most, but usually they are no more techno-savvy than any other staff member. The real difference is their open-mindedness, their willingness to try new things, to be curious about the world and how it works, and to always be thinking about how they can impart this sense of curiosity to their students.

Curiosity is an important trait when working with technology in a classroom because technology is an area that is constantly changing. Some people find this rapid change disconcerting and difficult to deal with, but it opens up great possibilities for learning. As we move further into the twenty-first century, it is becoming obvious that the key currencies of the new digital age are creativity, innovation, out-of-the-box thinking and the ability to come up with interesting solutions. These traits all require a heightened sense of open-mindedness.

As we see new technologies, instead of just marvelling at how impressive they can be, we should try asking ourselves: 'How could I use this?' We should be willing to look beyond the world as we currently understand it, and begin to think of ways in which we can shape the world to be what we want it to be. New technologies are especially good at letting us do this.

As teachers, we need to get much better at being open-minded, creative and innovative because these form a core of the skills that we need to develop in our students if we are to do justice to their great potential for the future.

7 BE WILLING TO SHARE

One of the things that digital technology is powerfully good at is enabling the easy re-use and sharing of lesson materials. Lessons and resources developed in a digital format can be saved, stored and archived for later use, which can be a great help in many different situations. Some examples are discussed below.

- **A number of classes in the same subject, all studying the same topic.** The teacher or teachers of those classes can develop a set of common lessons that can then be delivered in a consistent way, ensuring that all students are exposed to the same information. Having lessons stored as complete digital packages that contain notes, pictures, videos, worksheets or whatever other resources are appropriate means that all classes get access to the same set of core materials for covering the base curriculum.
- **A series of lessons that are taught every year.** The ability to save lessons means they can be developed once and re-used many times. Naturally, some things will change each year and there will probably need to be some updating of the content to reflect those changes, but the core of the lessons will often stay the same. This re-use of lessons from year to year, even if just for a single teacher, can be a big timesaver.
- **Shared lesson development.** In situations where more than one teacher is teaching the same year group, one teacher may choose to develop one unit of work while another teacher develops a different unit of work. In some situations, this may be simpler and less time consuming than having both teachers work together to develop both units—although the collaborative element can also be a great benefit.

Once developed, these units can then be exchanged and shared between both teachers, reducing the overall workload on individuals.

- **Collective lesson development.** In the same way that a wiki enables a group of people to work on the same document at the same time, digital lessons can be developed collaboratively by a group of teachers. In fact, online collaborative tools such as a wiki or a GoogleDoc can be an outstanding way for busy teachers to brainstorm together and develop the core ideas for a series of lessons around a topic or theme. These group-developed documents can then be transformed into digital lessons using either the IWB's proprietary flipbook-style software or whatever other digital resources might be appropriate. The important thing is that lessons and learning paths can be designed by a team of teachers rather than single individuals, not only spreading the workload but also fostering collaboration, teamwork and shared thinking.

- **National sharing.** Despite the fact that school systems differ slightly in their syllabus requirements, there is still a great deal of overlap. As more countries move closer to a national curriculum, the idea of sharing resources, not only between teachers in the same school but between different schools across the nation, makes much more sense. For example, why should a teacher in Perth, Australia develop a complete unit of work around a topic that a teacher on the east coast in Brisbane had already created? It makes so much more sense to pool our collective resources and ideas rather than persisting with the endless 're-invention of the wheel', which teachers are so used to doing. Every teacher has muttered that phrase about re-inventing the wheel at some point, and the development of digital lessons offers a truly workable solution to that problem.

- **Global sharing.** Taking things a step further, there is no reason why lesson ideas cannot be shared on a global scale. With so many teachers now connected and forming communities via the Internet, the possibilities and opportunities for sharing beyond individual geographical boundaries of time and place have melted away.

8 BE PREPARED TO PLAN

It is imperative in a digital school, where the use of digital technology is woven into the everyday operations of all parts of the school, that the effective use of technology is factored into the school's overall development plan. Do not have a separate ICT plan or (heaven forbid!) a special 'IWB plan'. It all needs to be part of a much bigger vision that is completely embedded into all the other parts of the way the school works (Lee & Gaffney, 2008). What history clearly reveals is that when schools have a separate, stand-alone plan for technology, they ultimately come up with yet another ineffectual 'bolt on' program that ends up not being integrated into the overall culture of the school.

The OECD made the telling observation in 2002 when it concluded:

> ICT implementation at a school level should be viewed in the context of school improvement plans and not simply as a technical issue. Problems that the school faces should be identified, strategies for overcoming these problems designed, and progress indicators designated. The highest returns on ICT in education appear to come when ICT is seen as part of a strategy for solving an important problem rather than as an end within itself.

> Venezky & Davis, 2002, p. 46

And yet, despite the logic of this, education authorities and schools continue to repeat the failings of history.

Your education authority might insist that the principal provide a school ICT plan purely to meet its documentation requirements, but good principals ought to be smart enough to know how to meet that obligation without it getting in the way of the real planning.

Implementation strategy

Allied to the holistic development plan is the need to have a comprehensive implementation strategy and an associated plan that addresses the range of human, organisational and technical variables that need attention in order to achieve the desired long-term embedding of technology across the curriculum. It is important that the plan focuses first and foremost on enriching the quality of teaching and the effectiveness of student learning, and then on specifics of the tools and support required. The school's strategy should be very much about teachers, students and human capital, enhancing the instructional program and refining the organisation, as well as installing and supporting the teaching tools. (A hint: When you write your plan, opt for a title like '21st Century Teaching' or 'e-Teaching 21' ... Call it what you like, but please don't refer to it as the 'IWB rollout'. That would focus on all the wrong things!)

Historically, most government and education authority instructional technology plans have focused on getting hardware and equipment into schools so that government officials can boast about how wonderful they are. This is a big mistake. Improved learning outcomes do not come as a result of more computers or more IWBs; and yet for many in authority this is always seen as the measuring stick for success. Throwing money at the problem will not help if that money is not being used wisely.

Once hardware goes into schools, the implementation is usually left to those who maintain the technology. This is a classic case of the inmates running the asylum, and it should come as no real surprise to discover that style of implementation strategy usually fails to achieve any real degree of whole-staff acceptance or a measurable improvement in teaching (Lee & Winzenried, 2009). While it is important for the principal to oversee any major implementation within a school, the research very strongly supports the idea of having a senior educator with good people and management skills to act as a project manager. These are the people who need to be given the responsibility, and the necessary time, to coordinate the school's implementation program.

CHAPTER 6

DESIGNING LESSONS

In many ways, the role of a teacher in the twenty-first century has evolved away from being the 'source of all knowledge' to being more of an 'information architect' charged with the task of designing engaging learning pathways for their students. This idea of the teacher as a designer of learning makes the job of teaching so much more than simply managing the flow of pre-made information from textbook to student. It means that teachers need to work alongside students to design tasks that will lead them through the process of meaningful learning; that teachers must tailor course content to the individual needs and interests of their students; that learning outcomes, task design, assessment planning (both formative and summative), and evaluation and redesign of curriculum are all central to the evolving craft of working with students to help them become their best.

Hopefully by now you are seeing the opportunities that IWBs offer in helping to deliver these learning pathways, and are keen to get your own board up and running. There are plenty of places on the web where you can get lesson ideas or even download ready-made lessons, and it is well worth spending some time looking through these online collections in order to see techniques that other teachers are using to engage their students. For many teachers there will come a point at which they will probably want to either modify these lessons or start creating their own from scratch. All teachers have their own style, their own way of explaining things and their own way of engaging student interest. So it is almost inevitable that you, too, will eventually want to start designing your own digital lessons.

This book takes the stance that, regardless of what brand of IWB teachers use, there are core features common to almost every board that can be utilised to build effective digital lessons. These features form the basic tools for working with interactive technology, and by thinking in terms of how a teacher can use these core features to 'tell their story' it encourages a focus on the pedagogy of lesson design.

There is a temptation, especially with newer users, to want specific examples of how to use these tools; for example, science or maths teachers might ask to see specific examples of how other science or maths teachers use the boards. But it is important to think beyond just narrow examples and typical uses. IWBs are extremely flexible tools and it would be a mistake to focus too heavily on specific examples of how they get used. The way a kindergarten teacher uses the IWB tools to teach the students is likely to be very different to the way a high school history teacher uses them; middle school art teachers will probably use the boards in very different ways to middle school geography teachers. And, therefore, the way you use the boards may be quite different depending on whether you are working with a group of special needs students or a group of highly gifted students. Every situation—and every teacher in those situations—will likely use the interactive technology in very different ways; and yet the lessons created by all these teachers will likely draw upon the same core set of features and techniques.

This makes it very hard to come up with 'one size fits all' descriptions or advice on how best to use IWBs. Just as different artists create very different artworks from the same six basic colours, or different musicians compose uniquely different pieces from the same twelve basic notes, so too will different teachers come up with very different ways of conveying concepts and ideas to their students by using the handful of core features built into the standard IWB software. In this chapter we take a look at some of the core tools that come with most IWBs and think about ways they can be used to build our own digital lessons. Rather than thinking in terms of step-by-step instructions, let us think instead about why these core tools exist and how we can master them to create beautiful works of art in our own teaching.

MAKING THE MOST OF 'DRAGABILITY'

If there is one feature that really sets interactive whiteboards apart from any other instructional technology, it is the ability to move objects around the screen by dragging them with a finger or a stylus. The ability of a user, be it teacher or student, to come to the board and physically drag an object from one place to another is one of the defining features of interactive technology.

It sounds almost too simple. Why would something as simple as being able to drag objects around a screen form such a fundamental aspect of IWB usage? Probably because the ability to physically move an object around a screen forms the very basis of interactivity. Dragging requires us to interact with the surface of the board in a very tactile way. When we combine this human touch with the almost magical ability of a computer to handle multiple media types, it creates a powerful combination. We can combine all the amazing possibilities of digital media with all the human qualities of good teaching.

Like so many aspects of teaching with an IWB, none of this should come as a surprise. Many good teachers have long used things like puzzles, jigsaws, models, words written on pieces of cardboard and so on to help make concepts easier to understand for their students. The basic idea behind dragging an object around on an IWB is conceptually no different from the way a teacher might press a blob of Blu-tack onto a card containing a word and then ask the student to stick it onto the wall below the correct picture. Likewise, the teacher who presents the students with a set of cards with words written on them and then asks the students to move them around on a desk to form sentences is using exactly the same idea. These simple 'drag and match' exercises are techniques that many teachers use regularly and effectively.

This notion of dragability is a key to IWB use. Some teachers seem to understand the importance of dragability the very first time they use an IWB, and some take a bit longer, but the concept of being able to drag objects around the screen is so fundamental to good IWB use that it could probably be seen as one of the indicators that the teacher understands the basic concept of interactivity and is moving on to the next phase of learning how to use an IWB. Without dragability, an IWB is just a very expensive conventional teaching board.

So, if you do nothing else, learn to design lessons that take advantage of dragability! Look at what you do right now in your conventional classroom that involves students moving, sorting, classifying or matching things. Whether it is labelling the bones in a human skeleton, adding musical notes to a staff, sorting a collection of words into nouns and verbs, classifying artwork into different categories, assembling parts of an image to make a complete picture, matching a word with its definition, or any similar tasks that we ask our students to do on a regular basis, think about how many of these are fundamentally about connecting ideas and moving an object from where it is to where it needs to be.

Some people will argue that a data projector on its own is just as effective as an IWB. At first it sounds like a believable argument, but the effective use of dragable objects is probably the main differentiator. We have talked about this elsewhere in the book, but, essentially, the act of physically coming to the board, reaching out and instinctively grabbing the thing that needs moving and dragging it to a new location so that it connects with another idea, is a critical differentiating advantage of an IWB.

UNDERSTANDING LAYERS

Strongly linked to the dragability of objects is the ability to place them in carefully ordered layers. Layering objects is another fundamental indicator of effective IWB use.

'Layering' refers to the way objects created on the board can be stacked in a particular order so that one object is able to obscure the object below it. Generally, the most recently created object sits at the top of the stack, but its position can be shuffled up or down the stack as required. So—as a simple example—a picture of a cow could be used to cover the word 'cow' and a student or teacher could drag the picture out of the way to reveal the text below. This principle of hiding and revealing by covering information with a layer above is a very common and extremely useful way to use the IWB interactively.

The numbers of ways this simple idea of hide-and-reveal can be used are almost limitless. Good teaching is often about telling a story, unfolding complexity with the students in order to make difficult ideas easy to understand. To do this, we sometimes need to reveal an idea a little at a time, perhaps covering the key words or images and revealing them in some sort of logical order.

Not all IWBs handle layering the same way. For example, the SMART Notebook and Interwrite Workbook allow a single stack of objects to be layered over each other as needed. Promethean's ActivStudio software has a slightly more complex layering model, with three different levels of stacking—background, middle layer and top layer. Objects can be stacked within each of these different layers, so that an object at the top of the middle layer is still behind an object at the bottom of the top layer. This can be a little confusing at first but does allow for some quite sophisticated uses of layering.

The main point is that all IWB flipbook-style software supports layering and that layering forms an important part of building teaching resources using this type of software.

AN UNLIMITED NUMBER OF SAVABLE SCREENS

Conventional teaching boards suffer from a number of major limitations, but one of the most obvious ones is the restricted amount teachers can put—and leave—on them. After scribbling notes and diagrams all over the board you have to then clear it again in order to continue, and everything you just scribbled is lost forever. Every teacher has written or drawn things on a conventional board, paused for the class to take it all in and then attempted to erase them in order to carry on with the lesson … only to be met with the usual barrage of 'Please! Don't rub it off yet, I haven't finished!' This makes it hard to keep the lesson flowing along; and once erased, it is impossible to go back and review something that is no longer there, although many times it would have been very handy.

Dedicated IWB software is generally based on a series of screens that can be flipped as individual pages. (On a SMART Board these screens are referred to as a 'notebook', Interwrite call theirs a 'workbook', Easiteach uses the term 'easibook' and Promethean refer to theirs as a 'flipchart'; and since we don't want to show favouritism we will refer to them as 'flipbooks'.) This simple idea that the teaching board has unlimited space is a powerful one. It encourages us to rethink the way we pace the delivery of content. It invites us to chunk content into much smaller bites and then simply flip to the next page, rather than trying to cram it all onto one screen. It also provides a less linear pathway through that information because the previous screens do not disappear and can be revisited at any point in a lesson.

The fact that these screens of information can be saved is also powerful. Lessons can be kept and reused for other classes, stored for use next year, or shared with other teachers. Students' interactions with the board can be retained for record keeping or used to review and compare for progress. Great ideas can be easily captured mid-lesson. Notes, ideas, diagrams and everything else that takes place during class time can be saved and then distributed to students and other teachers in the form of the original software, or converted to PDF, Flash, PowerPoint or a number of other easy-to-use formats. This simple option to save (so much a part of working with digital files) is something that was never available when using conventional teaching boards and yet it opens up so many options.

A WIDE RANGE OF PEN AND HIGHLIGHTER TOOLS

There has always been enormous power in being able to present ideas to a group in the form of words and pictures. The sheer simplicity of being able to do this is probably what has made the faithful chalkboard such a cornerstone of classrooms all over the world for so many years. While this book certainly advocates interactive whiteboards as a far better and more flexible alternative to the teaching boards of old, to dismiss the importance of being able to make notes and draw diagrams to share with a class would be doing the humble chalkboard a great disservice. So do not lose sight of the fact that you can still use your IWB for something as mundane as 'just writing'.

Some may point out that an old-fashioned chalkboard (or conventional whiteboard) is quicker and simpler to write on in an ad hoc way, but when the advantages of virtual pens with their variety of colours, thickness and transparency levels are taken into account, there is much more that they enable you to do. Also, virtual pens do not get misplaced and they never run out of ink, and anything written with a virtual pen can be saved and reused again.

IWB pens can be used to write over other sources, annotating images and maps, highlighting text on web pages, calling out important sentences or using arrows to explain the flow of an idea. They can be used to underline the verbs in a sentence, circle the important numbers in a table of data, or draw an army's invasion route on a map. Younger students can use the pen tools to practise and demonstrate their writing skills to the class; and students of any age seem to enjoy coming out to the board and using the pen to write, draw or highlight information. While impressive interactivity and learning objects might be the dazzlers when you see an IWB being used for the first time, do not underestimate the powerful ways in which the humble pen can be used on an IWB.

On some boards, the 'pen' can also be just a finger. There is some debate by the different IWB manufacturers as to whether having actual pens is better than being able to draw with a finger. Some will argue that students need to learn to write using a pen and that a finger is clearly not ideal for teaching students to form letters correctly. While there may be some truth to this, most finger-driven boards can also be operated with a pen, so it becomes something of a moot point—although it is true that softboards only allow a single point of contact, forcing users to avoid resting their hand on the board's surface as they write and therefore writing in a less natural way. The counter-argument says that the tactile experience of interacting with the surface using nothing but a finger is a great advantage and does not 'ruin' the students' ability to write with a pen, since writing on a board and writing on a flat surface are fundamentally quite different experiences. As always, there are pros and cons and the best suggestion is to try both systems to see what works best for you.

Many IWBs also offer some form of handwriting recognition tool capable of transforming handwritten script into fully editable font-based text. This feature usually is used far more in IWB sales demonstrations than on a day-to-day basis in the classroom; however, the possibility is there and some teachers and students make good use of this tool.

INSTANT SCREEN CAPTURES WITH THE CAMERA TOOL

Nearly all IWB software has the ability to take a snapshot of whatever is on the screen and then immediately dump it into a flipbook, ready to be shown, annotated, arranged and interacted with. This is typically quick and simple, so that grabbing an image, a piece of text, a table of data, etc. can be done 'on the fly' and instantly dropped into a lesson. While the camera snapshot tool is very handy for preparing lessons and offers an easy way to add resources to a flipbook in advance, its real power lies in the ability to quickly grab text and images. If you can see it on your screen, the camera tool can grab it and bring it into your lesson immediately for showing, sharing and discussing. For example, have you spotted an image on the Internet that illustrates a point well? Use the camera tool to grab it and import it into your lesson. Show, annotate and mark up photographs, diagrams, artwork, maps and charts. Then, using the pen and highlighter tools, you and your students can add to and interact with these images, circling key features, tracing over important sections and helping to deepen understandings of key visual ideas. Or use the camera tool to take text from other sources, snapshot it and drop it into a flipbook for annotation. Whether poetry, prose, news articles, music scores, web pages, quotes … just find it, snapshot it and use it.

Of course, none of this is revolutionary. Teachers have always used resources that can be shown to students using technologies like wall posters or overhead projectors (OHPs). For example, teachers have always been able to show information to students on a big screen using an OHP and an OHP pen to annotate and write over that information. Most teachers would probably agree that the ability to present an article or image to the class and interact with it by writing over it is an extremely useful technique. The downside of OHP transparencies is that they can be time consuming to prepare, must usually be done in advance of the lesson, are typically limited to black and white, require significant effort to erase and reuse, and require physical duplication to share with multiple teachers. What the IWB can do is to provide the same sort of functionality with the added benefits of full-colour imagery, non-destructive saving, simple sharing and storage, ease of reuse and—perhaps most significant of all—allowing these snapshots to be created immediately if needed.

This comes back to one of our key ideas. Used well, an interactive whiteboard provides all the advantages that traditional teaching tools have always offered, yet it offers layers of additional functionality that can open up entirely new opportunities for learning in new ways—if only we take advantage of them.

DIGGING INTO THE GALLERY

How many times have you been preparing a worksheet or some notes for a class and wanted to include a particular piece of clip art, diagram or photo? Products like Microsoft Office with its web-enabled clip art search can be a great tool for finding suitable images to include in documents. Typically, these sorts of documents are created in advance, before class time.

On most interactive boards, the same sort of access to a large library of clip-art type images also exists, but this usually extends to include photos, background images, videos, sounds, shapes, lines and interactive simulations. These collections—usually referred to as a library or gallery—typically contain thousands of useful objects that can help teachers to prepare lessons in advance and can be accessed easily and immediately during a lesson.

Are you in the middle of a lesson and suddenly need a map of the world to show your students where something is? You can probably find that map in the library. Do you need a drawing of a test tube or a Bunsen burner? A symbol for a battery or for a resistor? An image of a 50-cent piece? How about a diagram of a soccer field? Or the sound of a cow mooing? Or a video clip of a butterfly emerging from a cocoon? Do you need a visual way to show how gears work? The chances are that you can find all of these and much more in your IWB's built-in library collection.

Most IWB resource libraries contain thousands of such resources that are structured around standard school curricula. This is important because it means that, unlike a general clip art collection, your IWB resource library is far more likely to have educationally useful things. So take the time to dig through the library/gallery supplied with your board and become familiar with it so you know what is in there. The big advantage is not merely that it contains many resources; it is how easily these resources can be accessed during a lesson when you need them.

A word of advice: learn to use the search function. When you start using the library, it is normal to want to browse through it. It is an intuitive way to hunt around and leads to all sorts of discoveries. However, the best method is to use 'Search', not 'Browse'. Each image in the library is (or should be) tagged with metadata—that is, information about itself—so that a search for the word 'australia' will return all the resources in the library tagged with that word, including maps, images of flags, photographs of Australian animals and plants, recordings of the national anthem and so on. Naturally, you can limit your search to specific media types if you prefer.

Finally, don't forget that the library is not static. You can add your own images, sounds, videos, etc. to the library collection, making it even more functional for meeting your specific needs. Images of school crests and logos, photos of students, digital images taken on a field trip, recordings of student or teacher voices can all be useful additions to the library that enable you easy access when you need them.

ADDING MEDIA TO THE MIX

One of the biggest differentiators between interactive board technology and anything that existed before it is the ease with which media can be included in a lesson. Whether that means including sound files linked to words so that language students can hear a word's pronunciation, or embedding a video clip so that students can analyse a movie scene's lighting and how it affects the mood, or the ability to drop a photo or a piece of audio or video into a lesson, it can dramatically change the entire dynamic of how students learn.

Again, none of this is new in the big sense. Teachers have always employed the use of media in their work. Photographs around the room, posters on the wall, use of audio cassette tapes or CDs and, of course, the use of television to show videos and DVDs have all been an intrinsic part of the teaching landscape for many years. To say that IWBs have enabled the use of different media forms into a classroom would therefore be misleading and untrue. What IWBs have done, however, is to aggregate these media forms, which have typically required various devices to use them, into an easy-to-manipulate digital format that can be accessed through a single point of contact.

In addition, because of the nature of digital resources, there is great flexibility in the way media types can be handled. Photographs can be zoomed into, audio can be stopped and started, video can be edited into relevant snippets—all far more easily than when these media forms existed in their old analogue forms. For example, high school English teachers are increasingly using film to teach literature. It is not uncommon to have students read a book and also watching the film of the book, selecting particular scenes from the film to analyse in detail. Doing this with a videotape or even a DVD is not so easy ... locating the scene, pausing at certain points in the action, rewinding to dissect the dialogue or action should be simple to do, but generally are not and can consume far more teaching time than they should. In addition, it can often be useful to compare a scene from one film with a scene from another, looking at similarities and differences. Juggling two or three DVDs during a lesson in order to find the scenes to compare can waste enormous chunks of class time, and many teachers would consider even attempting to do this more trouble than it is worth.

The same task on an IWB is relatively trivial because of the way computers treat digital media. There is obviously some preparation work to do before the lesson, identifying the required scenes and using software editing tools to isolate that footage into the desired chunks. But once this is done, these chunks of video can easily be stored on the computer or dropped into a flipbook page, ready to show the class. Students are able to watch the clips, stop, start, pause, rewind, compare and annotate with almost no fiddling about, trying to find the correct place on the tape or disk. This makes for a far more focused lesson, with more time spent on the task of actually learning the important ideas around the literature and less time fiddling with the technicalities of managing DVDs.

CHAPTER 7

BETTER ON THE BIG SCREEN

So far, much of our discussion has centred on the use of the flipbook-style software that comes with most interactive whiteboards. However, it would be a big mistake to think that this was the only (or even the main) way to use the board. There are plenty of other very effective ways to use an IWB that have nothing at all to do with self-created or pre-prepared flipbooks, but rather with simply tapping into the big range of existing software applications that are already being used on standard personal computers.

Some of this software might be used by students independently on individual classroom computers, but can also be used in a group setting around an interactive whiteboard. It would be almost logical to conclude that using regular software on an IWB is an acceptable alternative to getting all students in front of their own computers. It might seem that giving each student access to their own computer is the ideal situation, and for many constructivist learning situations this may certainly be the case. But the IWB is not a second-rate alternative to taking the class to the computer room. Contrary to this notion, this chapter makes the suggestion that there is plenty of standard personal computer software that can in fact be even more effective when used in a group situation on an IWB. It asserts that good teachers are able to use standard software applications and leverage their ability to unpack difficult concepts, guide students into discussions that consider alternative points of view and uncover hidden insights that otherwise may have remained undiscovered.

There is a great deal of high-quality software available these days. Some of it is available as commercial products, while an increasing number are freely available as Open Source products or Web 2.0 applications that live online. Part of the job of a teacher in the twenty-first century is to recognise those applications that can be put to effective use in their classrooms. In this section we explore some of the software applications that run exceptionally well on an IWB because of the way they lend themselves to the group-teaching dynamic that IWBs support so well.

GOOGLE EARTH

[Mac/Windows—Free]

There is a general sense of awe the very first time one sees Google Earth being used on an interactive whiteboard. It is hard to imagine an application that could be more suited to the IWB environment. Google Earth is a detailed 3D model of the Earth built from an almost incomprehensible amount of real geographical data and satellite imagery. The program opens with our planet gently revolving in virtual space, inviting a user to reach out and touch it. Using a pen or finger, this globe can be rotated, spun and moved, zoomed in on and out of, and manipulated to show the Earth from any angle or view. It is an incredibly engaging experience. The satellite maps that cover the surface are real photographs and can be zoomed in to show detail that, in some places, clearly reveals vehicles and people on the ground. The surface of the globe is constructed with reasonably accurate height data, so a visit to the Grand Canyon or the Himalayan Mountains will be rendered in a full 3D view that can be rotated and zoomed to show a surprisingly good representation of the mountains and valleys. Some cities contain 3D models of buildings that sit atop their mapped location, many with photo-realistic 'skins' so they look almost real.

Figure 7.1 (page 90) shows New York's Manhattan Island for an amazing example of a major city.

As well as the core data that makes up the Google Earth experience, there are a number of layers that can be turned on and off to overlay additional data on the map. Layers that show buildings, roads, geographical boundaries, names and labels all contribute to the information available. Beautiful photographs from National Geographic and Gigapixel, informative videos from YouTube, amazing high-resolution images from Panoramio are just a few of the layers that can be turned on to reveal much more. Google also recently added a feature called Street View that enables a viewer to zoom in on a city street then look around in a 360-degree panorama, seeing buildings, cars, shops and sometimes even people.

Figure 7.1 Exploring New York City with Google Earth

(Reprinted with permission from The Sanborn Map Company, Inc. © The Sanborn Map Company, Inc. 2009. All rights reserved.)

Using the IWB, students can explore the Earth's surface to reveal far more than was ever possible with a paper atlas or a plastic globe. For example, let's say a class is working on a thematic unit of work on Antarctica. Using Google Earth, the Earth can be rotated to show Antarctica from any angle, looking directly down above the South Pole, or zoomed in to explore the Ross Ice Shelf or McMurdo Base. Turning on the appropriate layers reveals a surprising number of geo-located photographs and videos to provide detailed insights into life on the frozen continent. Prior to tools like Google Earth students would have been limited to a few images in books from the library or sitting as a whole class and passively watching a video about Antarctica. Combining Google Earth's interactivity with the physical manipulation made possible by the IWB, students can now move from place to place, focus on landforms of interest, zoom in to see detail or zoom out to get the big picture. They can spin the globe around to compare the northern Arctic region, seeing exactly how it differs from the Antarctic south and how one is a continental landmass while the other is a frozen icecap. They can overlay Antarctica with map data taken at a different time and compare, say, an aerial photo taken in the 1970s with current satellite images; these layers can be overlaid on each other and turned on and off to investigate the possible effects of climate change.

As you can imagine, the flexibility and depth of data available with a tool like Google Earth opens up entirely new possibilities for a classroom. Curious students are able to not only wonder about some aspect of the planet, but then actually go and look at it, perhaps answering their own question but probably raising many more in the process. It is this endless well of interesting data that can feed the curiosity of even the most inquisitive students that provides not only physical interactivity with the board but, more importantly, an intellectual interactivity that engages directly with the thinking process.

Although an unstructured use of Google Earth can be a lot of fun for students, it remains to be seen whether they would get full value from it without appropriate guidance and wisdom of a teacher. Using Google Earth in a computer lab setting with the students sitting at their own computers could easily descend into a free-for-all that, although interesting, might not lead the students through the sorts of concepts they need to actually learn. In many situations, the use of Google Earth and other tools like it can be far more effective and valuable when used in a group setting with an interactive whiteboard.

It turns out that in many situations, the IWB is not just an alternative to each student having access to their own computer, but it can actually be a much better option for enabling effective learning and teaching in a group situation.

GOOGLE SKETCHUP

[Mac/Windows/Linux—Free]

SketchUp is another amazing tool from Google that works incredibly well on an IWB. Its main purpose is to create 3D shapes that can be manipulated and moved around in space. From simple objects like cubes, cylinders and cones through to far more complicated objects like buildings and cars, SketchUp uses a simple model of extruding complex 3D shapes from very simple 2D shapes. For example, if one wants to create a cube, one simply draws a flat rectangle on the ground and then pulls it up vertically to give it height. Other shapes are created in similar ways and pushed, pulled, sliced, moved and grouped to create as complex a shape as needed. It is an easy-to-understand method for creating 3D shapes that have typically been quite complex to build using other methods.

Once created, the virtual spaces that these shapes live in can easily be navigated with the cursor so that dragging around an object enables the viewer to see it from any angle and level of zoom. Virtual houses can be built that can then be virtually explored, or zoomed out from to show how it looks from street level. There are enormous possibilities. On a large IWB screen, this fluid motion through 3D space can be quite a stunning visual effect and usually draws lots of 'oohs' and 'aahs' from anyone seeing it for the first time.

Although students can have a lot of fun learning to create their own 3D models, there is also a great deal of merit in using a tool like SketchUp in a student-centred—but teacher-led—group situation. Maths teachers might use SketchUp to communicate ideas about shapes and solids, creating cones and cylinders and asking students to come to the board and manipulate them, exploring them from different angles and views. The surface of objects can be created out of a variety of simulated materials. For example, a cylinder could be made of glass, making it much easier to visualise the entire shape from any angle. SketchUp also enables the use of cutting planes, so a 3D shape could be sliced to expose its cross-section. These are all concepts that are difficult for many students to visualise in their heads but fairly easy to grasp if they can manipulate a virtual model.

As well as the shapes we create ourselves, there is also a big library of pre-built models available online. SketchUp users all over the world spend countless hours creating accurate virtual models of things like buildings and bridges built as scaled replicas of real-world buildings and bridges, and then upload them to Google's online gallery. One of the main purposes of these structures is to populate the cities in Google Earth, and there is strong integration between the two products. It also means that anyone can browse through the online gallery and download an accurate pre-built model, open it in SketchUp and then explore it in 3D space. So, for example, a group of students may be studying a unit of work on bridges, looking at different types of bridges, trusses and engineering principles. In a few clicks, accurate scale models of the Sydney Harbour Bridge, the Golden Gate Bridge and the London Bridge can all be pulled up on the IWB and explored (see Figure 7.2). Using a finger or a pen, the structures can be rotated and viewed from all angles, zoomed in on to reveal the design of the trusses and beams, and so on. Students can stand on the deck level of the bridge, or fly to the highest point, getting a unique opportunity to explore in a way that would not be possible otherwise. So much is possible in a virtual 3D environment.

Figure 7.2 Virtual model of the Sydney Harbour Bridge

(Courtesy: Google SketchUp)

Just like Google Earth, although there can be great value in getting students to explore this world on their own, it can be equally powerful to explore it together as a teacher-led group on a single large screen. Students enjoy coming to the board and moving around in 3D, and the group becomes highly engaged in the process. The teacher is still present to guide, prompt and provoke the students with questions, lead the discussion and point out essentials in a way that both students and teacher may never discover on their own. Students still do the work of discussing and interacting and learning, but the group situation around a shared screen can be very effective.

Again, it is worth highlighting the role of the IWB in this situation. We can have an inquisitive group of students engaging with a digital environment that is extremely immersive, guided by a wise adult who leads them through the process of learning the things that may be important. Compare this with the alternative ways of doing a similar lesson: in a computer lab situation, this session could easily become big on fun but low on actual learning; in a regular classroom, this would usually be a paper-based activity done with worksheets or static posters.

Neither of these situations is ideal. The IWB in this case acts as a conduit for linking the teacher with the learners as they share the learning in an explicit but fun way.

SKYPE

[Mac/Windows/Linux—Free]

Skype is a way to make voice and video calls between computers. It also enables text chats between computers. And it can even make voice calls from a computer to a real telephone. All of this makes it an extremely potent tool for learning in the classroom.

Classrooms have typically been places of relative isolation; yet, ironically, students and teachers work inside their classroom every day trying to learn about the real world outside. Traditionally, the way a classroom deals with making a connection to the outside world is to go on an excursion or field trip so that students get an opportunity to see and experience life beyond the classroom. Alternatively, the world could come to them in the form of a guest speaker who visits the school to share their perspectives. Both of these options provide wonderful opportunities to reach out beyond the classroom walls and often become highlights of a student's school experience.

But how often does this happen? Once or twice a year? Perhaps once a term if you are lucky? Wouldn't it be wonderful if we could somehow give our students more exposure to this big world beyond the classroom; to let them connect with outside experts on a more regular basis? Skype lets us do that.

Skype is not the sort of software that we would typically install on every student computer. There are many reasons why giving students their own personal access to Skype is not a good idea. (There are some compelling reasons why we might do it, too, but that becomes an entirely different proposition.) However, Skype works particularly well on an interactive whiteboard in a group situation. The use of Skype on a teacher's computer projected on the IWB opens up incredible opportunities for connecting the class to the outside world.

Consider a class getting a virtual visit from a book author. The teacher makes contact with the author in advance to arrange the call. At a designated time the class is able to sit in front of the IWB and chat in real time with the author. The author might talk about their book and the characters and some of the ideas behind them. Students can hear and see the author on the screen and, most importantly, ask questions and converse with him or her. It becomes a conversation rather than a lecture. Students might ask for clarification about the plot, give an opinion about a character or just ask the author about some of their experiences. The author gets a chance to connect with the readers.

The opportunity to go directly to the source of information like this is invaluable for students. Think about the doors this opens—business studies students talking to bank managers; history students chatting with people that fought in a war; sports science students engaged in dialogue with Olympic athletes; art students asking questions of practising artists … the possibilities are endless. And what about using Skype to connect to other classrooms; across the state; across the country; across the world, with groups of students working on projects together across the Internet? This is the stuff that engages students and captures their attention.

Moving beyond mere voice calls, Skype can support a full-screen video call if the participants have webcams on their computers. So students can sit and talk face-to-face with their virtual visitors, asking questions and discussing key ideas, with the visitor's image projected onto the IWB—the next best thing to actually having them in the room. There are also extra plug-in facilities for Skype that allow calls to be recorded as audio files, opening up some great options for using these interviews in student-produced podcasts or multimedia productions. Imagine, for example, talking to an artist about their work and later using the recording of the call as a soundtrack to a photo slideshow of the artist's work.

The Skype–IWB environment has so much to offer a classroom full of learners.

Cynics will point out that the IWB is not actually contributing much in this situation beyond acting as a screen, and that the same value could be gained from a data projector alone. And they would be correct, of course. The point, however, is that without the IWB in the room the projector would almost certainly never have been there in the first place. Until IWBs came along, there were almost no classrooms anywhere (outside of a computer lab perhaps) that had a permanently installed digital projector in place. So the opportunities to even ponder these sorts of shared large-screen experiences were almost non-existent. This highlights again the 'Trojan horse' effect that IWBs have had in bringing powerful digital technologies into mainstream classrooms.

GEOGEBRA

[Mac/PC/Linux (Java based)—Free]

GeoGebra is a free dynamic geometry software that allows the user to drag points, lines, shapes and curves with a 'mouse' on a flat Cartesian plane. Every object has both a geometric and algebraic representation in the geometry and algebra windows respectively. When an object is dragged in the geometry window, its algebraic representation also changes. This ability to visually manipulate mathematical objects makes it ideally suited for use on an interactive whiteboard. Students can visualise and understand maths concepts more clearly because they can investigate the relationship between the geometry and algebra of an object in a dynamic, tactile context.

GeoGebra can be used to investigate plotting points, gradients of lines, properties of triangles, polygons, circles, circle geometry theorems, calculus concepts and so on. Because these concepts can be relatively abstract, some students find them difficult to understand, and too often students learn them through the rote memorisation of formulas that fail to achieve any real long-term understanding, even though the student might pass the test at the end. GeoGebra's strength is that it allows students to dynamically investigate mathematical concepts in an algebraic and geometric context. Because students can change the shape or position of a geometric object and see the algebraic representation change simultaneously, GeoGebra enables students to see mathematical concepts as 'living, breathing and moving', which offers them the opportunity to develop deeper understandings than the traditional method of seeing only static objects on a blackboard.

For example, using GeoGebra, three points could be created on the IWB and the angle measurements displayed in real time, so that if one of the points were moved the angle display would update. When you drag the points around the screen, you can actually see the measured angles between those points changing. This can be useful for exploring concepts like acute or obtuse angles. Taking this a step further, say you are trying to help students understand that the three angles of a triangle sum to 180 degrees. The three angles that make up the triangle could be displayed, along with the calculated total of the angles, adding up to 180 degrees. As students move any of the triangle's points around the screen they would be able to see the individual angle measurements change, but the calculated total of 180 would remain constant, making it easy to concretely see 'the angle sum of a triangle' in action. Students can see that this property is true for any triangle they choose to create simply by playing with the shape on the IWB.

Students are able to play 'what if' with ideas that might otherwise have remained quite abstract to them. A whole range of maths concepts can easily be explored in dynamic, graphical ways that were not possible using a traditional teaching board. GeoGebra even enables the creation of dynamic sliding controls that can be attached to a specific variable, such as an angle or a length. This makes it possible to set up a geometrical example and to manipulate the key variables by simply moving sliders around.

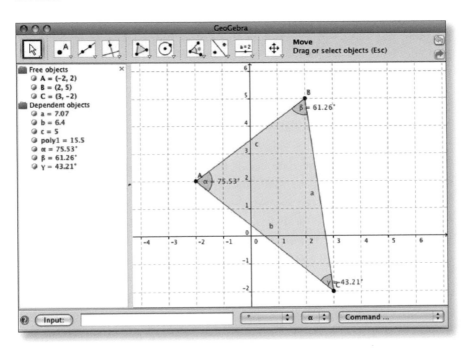

Figure 7.3 Manipulating angles in real time with GeoGebra

The advantage of this type of mathematical manipulation in a class setting using an IWB ought to be fairly apparent. Maths, especially in the high school years, is typically not an area that most students will learn effectively without a good deal of explicit teacher guidance. Of course, there still needs to be plenty of room for discussion and questioning by students so they feel engaged in the learning, but the wise guidance of a teacher is critical to learning most maths concepts. The IWB environment can deepen that learning process by providing a large interactive screen on which to actively and concretely manipulate ideas that are often quite abstract and difficult to grasp for many students.

Tools such as GeoGebra are a perfect example of why IWB technology is ideal for whole-class teaching and learning, and why some software applications truly are better on the big screen.

GAPMINDER WORLD

[Mac/PC/Linux (Web 2.0, Flash-based)—Free]

One of the powerful ways in which we can stimulate deep intellectual thinking in our students is by presenting them with data—sometimes in quite large amounts—and asking them to make sense of it. Some of the very best learning activities can happen when students need to wade through masses of raw data in order to draw conclusions about what that data might mean. In doing so, they often have to consider the cause-and-effect relationships inherent in that data, or think about what might happen if we were to look at that data in a slightly different way.

Gapminder World is a Flash-based online tool that contains a mind-boggling amount of raw data about the world. Collected by the United Nations, it contains up-to-date statistics about population, birth, death and infant mortality rates, carbon dioxide production, income per capita, and so on. It contains statistics about the world's health, wealth and education, including detailed breakdowns by age and gender. Although this information is all freely available from the UN, making sense of it without a tool like Gapminder World would be very difficult indeed.

The public face of Gapminder is a public health professor from Sweden named Hans Rosling, and he has produced a number of short videos that delve into many statistical truths about our world. Rosling is fond of saying that looking at statistics without some sort of visualisation tool is like trying to appreciate a beautiful piece of music just by looking at the notes.

Gapminder World essentially allows any set of statistics to be mapped against any other set of statistics. The results are represented by coloured circles representing the world's countries, and their size is usually set to represent population—so the bigger the circle, the bigger the population (see Figure 7.4). They are also colour-coded by region; so, all the African countries are shaded dark blue, Europe is another colour, and so on.

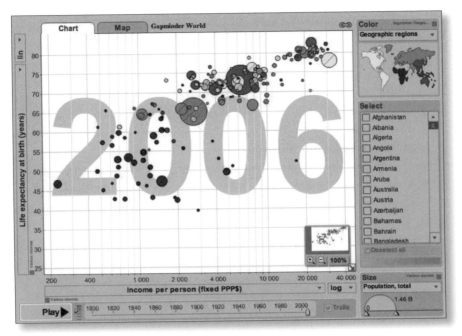

Figure 7.4 Exploring the world of statistics with Gapminder World

(Reprinted with permission from Gapminder, www.gapminder.org)

By mapping two sets of statistics against each other, say for example, average income per capita versus average lifespan, the relative relationships of the world's countries are presented on the graph, so notions such as 'the richer you are, the longer you live' can be explored.

Just that set of data alone could lead to some very interesting discussions in a classroom. It becomes easy to see whether the assumption is in fact correct. Students could theorise about why a person's life expectancy might be affected by how wealthy they are. Robust discussions can take place about the meaning of the two metrics, the possible cause-and-effect relationships contained within them, and what such a comparison might reveal between two very different countries such as Sweden and Zambia. However, changing the metrics is as simple as selecting them from a drop-down list and the graph instantly redraws to reflect the new data relationships. This opens enormous possibilities for learning!

Unlike trying to wade through masses of textual data, Gapminder makes it simple to explore and play 'what if'. Discussions in class—facilitated by a teacher but directed by the students—can uncover interesting relationships in the data and reveal stunning insights into our world. Students are free to ask questions and propose other comparisons and, providing the data is available, Gapminder makes those comparisons trivially simple to investigate.

But it goes further than that. Gapminder contains historical as well as current data. A slider along the bottom of the window allows a user to go back in time, looking at years and years of previous data. Now, patterns and trends can be dynamically analysed as well. The rapid industrialisation of countries like India and China can be clearly seen as their circles animate across the screen, corresponding to a growing rise in average income. Health trends in sub-Saharan Africa become obvious as the dark blue circles move across the screen, mapping child mortality rates over the years.

This is far more data than most students could comfortably make sense of on their own, which is why the role of a teacher is critical to facilitating and guiding these discussions. In a class setting, a group of learners gathered around an IWB and led by a wise teacher can be directed into conversations that uncover ideas about that information that may not otherwise be obvious to the students. Theories can be tested and assumptions can be challenged.

The IWB performs an important role in this setting. As a computer lab activity, with each student sitting in front of their own computer, there is a strong likelihood that most students would never uncover many of these relationships in a deep or meaningful way. With the guidance of a knowledgeable teacher, the shared group learning environment of a classroom, and the digital flexibility made possible with an IWB, the learning can be so much more powerful.

WITH WEB 2.0, THE LIST GOES ON ...

The above are just a few suggestions, but the list of software applications that work fantastically well on an IWB in a group environment could go on and on. Their effectiveness ultimately comes down to the teachers and their ability to leverage the interactivity inherent in the software tool and combine it with quality teaching techniques like effective questioning, good classroom management and the right kind of group dynamic.

A growing number of websites use technologies like Flash, Java and AJAX to create highly interactive sites that live on the Internet yet behave very much like programs one would normally need to install on one's computer. This explosion of Web 2.0 Internet applications that live 'in the cloud' is changing the game dramatically. The levels of interactivity made possible by these Web 2.0 technologies provide access to an ever-expanding range of software tools that work extremely well on an IWB, using nothing more complicated than a web browser such as Firefox or Internet Explorer. In many cases, by running the browser in full screen mode (usually by pressing the F11 button), online applications can be made to use the entire IWB screen and be almost imperceptible from software that would be installed on your hard drive.

For many IWB software tools, this means there may be a Web 2.0 alternative to the standard locally installed program. Mind mapping that would normally be done using an application like Inspiration or SMARTIdeas can equally be done using a Web 2.0 alternative such as Webspiration (www.mywebspiration.com) or Bubbl.us (www.bubbl.us). Timelines can be created using web applications like Dipity (www.dipity.com) or XTimeline (www.xtimeline.com).

There is no shortage of amazing Web 2.0 tools out there that work superbly in an IWB environment.

SHOW-AND-TELL FOR SOFTWARE TRAINING

The list of what software works on an interactive whiteboard is almost endless, since anything that works on your computer will work on the board. For years before IWBs were common, many teachers of information technology or computing studies had a projector in their classrooms and realised the benefits that a large display of their computer screen offered. Although the introduction of IWBs has brought many more teaching advantages to every subject and grade right across the school, its effectiveness for doing something as mundane as projecting what is on your computer screen is still extremely useful. The IWB is not essential for demonstrating how to do simple tasks such as showing the students how to create a page border in Microsoft Word, or how to include an attached photo file to an email, or how to use Wikipedia, but it sure makes it easier! Try teaching a complex computer application such as Adobe Flash or Photoshop without a large screen display at the front of the room and see how difficult it is. There are lots of computer-based operations that are ridiculously difficult to explain but quite trivial to demonstrate. Show is almost always better than tell.

In a computer lab situation, trying to teach a program like Flash can be quite difficult, especially if students have never seen it before. Explaining how to build multi-layered, timeline-based key frame animations can be hard to explain at the best of times, but trying to teach it without any visual aid to accompany the explanation is near impossible.

Ok, kids, to hide that layer, look up near the corner of your screen and click in the top section on the left where you see the little icon that looks like a pencil with a line through it ... No, not that icon, the other icon ... Yes, that one ... everyone see it?

It doesn't really work, does it?

Having a projector in a classroom improves the situation enormously, but it still means that the teacher is usually sitting down at a computer away from the screen, completely disembodied from the display.

Ok, kids, to hide the layer, click up here ... See where I'm wiggling my mouse ... and click on this button that looks like this ... (more wiggling of mouse) ... Can everyone see it?

Better, but hardly ideal.

For many veteran teachers of computing subjects who have had a projector attached to their computer for several years, the IWB is sometimes seen as a pointless accessory. These people are often the most cynical and hardest to convince about the benefits of the IWB. But even for something like teaching students how to use a piece of software, the IWB brings subtle but significant benefits. You no longer have to be a disembodied voice furiously wiggling your mouse for attention. You can point at the icons and menus with your finger or pen, having them react to your touch. You can make eye contact with your students rather than having your attention focused between your computer screen and the big screen. You can read the expressions and the body language of your students, monitoring for understanding and engagement. You can invite students to the board, even to take over the lesson. Students can be more involved in the learning process by taking on some of the teaching process.

Those teachers who cannot understand the benefits that the IWB brings to this sort of teaching need to try one for a while and then try going back to the old way of doing it. That is when one really notices the difference it makes. The IWB provides the connection between the act of teaching and the engaging digital resources that exist inside our computers. It brings them to a single large interactive space that all members of the class can share.

You get the idea by now. There are many, many amazing computer applications that were perhaps never designed for a classroom large-screen environment but happen to work extremely well in one. Flash-based learning objects, interactive websites, simulated virtual 3D worlds … all these things can be very effective on an IWB. Thinking about what they have in common, a few factors seem to keep coming up:

- They use 'dragability' as a fundamental feature. In all these applications, objects can easily be manipulated and moved around to create new views, new relationships and new situations.

- They provide an opportunity to play 'what if'. Good IWB software allows students to easily manipulate objects or data to test their theories about what difference those changes might make. Variables can be changed so that their effects can easily be observed.

- They allow data to be presented in ambiguous ways. Some of the best software is entirely open-ended in the way that it does not lead students to a 'right' answer but rather provides an environment for them to be challenged with multiple viewpoints, multiple possibilities and multiple 'right' answers.

- They often contain intellectual complexities or have a degree of depth such that students may not discover the real implications of the data they contain. Applications that are 'better on the big screen' are usually those that require the wise guidance of a teacher to help unpack their hidden gems—not so much technologically, but pedagogically.

- They are visually engaging. Let's face it, an application that looks 'cool' is nicer to use and captures the attention of students. Of course, it needs to do much more; just looking pretty is not enough by itself, but if the visual effects of an application can provide a 'wow' factor without becoming distracting then that can only be a good thing.

- They are intuitive to use. Nobody really wants to read instruction manuals or spend lots of time being trained in how to use a tool. A good tool should be immediately intuitive to figure out, or at least highly discoverable.

8

COME INTO MY CLASSROOM ...

In creating this chapter, we asked a number of leading educators to contribute a brief snapshot of how they use interactive technology. These educators, from all around the world, were asked to share some insights into and ideas about the ways in which they use their interactive whiteboards and how the IWB has become an embedded part of the learning that takes place within their classrooms. The snapshots are real-world examples (admittedly from teachers with a proven track record for using IWB technology successfully) on how their IWB fits into their daily teaching practice. Each snapshot gives an insight into the many ways that the technology can be used to deepen student learning and engagement.

When compiling these snapshots, a few things come through loud and clear. First, there is no one 'right' way to use IWB technology. These examples highlight the diversity of methods that each teacher uses to get value out of their board. Second, in all the examples it becomes quite obvious that the IWB is simply being used as an enabler for richer, deeper learning to take place. Student engagement, richness of understanding, creativity, teamwork and learning ... these qualities are patently evident in the examples. In every case, it is not about the technology per se; good teaching is always at the heart of what is taking place in these classrooms, and the IWB is acting as one of the enabling tools used to support that good teaching.

JESS McCULLOCH—HAWKESDALE, AUSTRALIA

Jess McCulloch teaches Chinese at Hawkesdale P12 College in country Victoria. She eagerly embraces the use of most educational technology and has a number of blog and wiki sites that she uses to engage her students more fully in the learning process.

Jess is a keen SMART Board user and has developed a number of innovative ways to use it for teaching languages. She also recently instigated the Interactive Whiteboard Challenge, where she used the power of the Internet to issue a number of weekly challenges to any teachers who wanted to take part. These challenges were designed to encourage other educators to explore their IWBs, regardless of make and model, and to push themselves to develop new skills and techniques for their effective use.

Jess noted in her interview:

One of my favourite things to use the interactive whiteboard for is creating audio translation and word find activities for my students. The interactive technology makes something that can be fairly bland—translation—into something my students can actually touch. To set up this activity, I make several short recordings in Audacity. Each word I need is a separate sound file. I then add these sound files to the whiteboard software, which in my case is Notebook because I have a SMART Board. When added to the software, the sound file (and MP3 file) is given an icon that looks a bit like a speaker. At this point I name each little speaker with the word that the recording says. My recordings are usually Chinese words, so naming each little file is another aspect of the resource that can be used. These speakers are now objects with a sound file attached and can be dragged from the content section onto the body of the file. Once they are there, you can just press them to hear the recording.

At this stage the files are ready for the activity. I usually ask two or three students to work on this activity together, while the rest of the groups are working on other things. Firstly, I drag out from the content folder a number of speaker icons and place them on one half of the board. I will stand to the side and ask them to translate a sentence for me; for example, 'I like to play basketball'. The students then need to go through the sound files and choose the right ones, put them in the right order and then play them for me. Another variation is to arrange many of the sound files randomly all over the board, say a word in English and ask the student to find the Chinese equivalent, creating an audio word find.

The interactive technology of the whiteboard allows my students to really get involved with the sounds of the words they are learning. It's great for those kinaesthetic learners who are often put off by written work. It allows kids to get out of their seats, and I have really noticed a keenness to be part of this activity. Students often find language learning threatening and difficult, but allowing students to interact with objects on the board has meant that, in their keenness to use the technology, they are also engaging with the Chinese words they think are so difficult. I have noticed that this particular activity and the use of the whiteboard in general have meant that a few students who are usually incredibly reluctant to give anything a go in Chinese class have willingly tried out things and consequently have been able to prove to themselves that they are capable and do know something.

The Whiteboard Challenge can be found online at http://white boardchallenge.wikispaces.com. Jess can be found online at www.techno lote.com.

TOM BARRETT—MIDLANDS, ENGLAND

Tom Barrett is a Year 5 teacher, ICT subject leader and assistant head teacher at Priestsic Primary and Nursery School in Nottingham. His school has had SMART Boards in every class since December 2003—from Nursery level to Year 6—and their use is an embedded part of the way the school works. Tom is well known for his work with IWBs as well as his use of collaborative technologies such as GoogleDocs and immersive multimedia tools like Google Earth. In addition to his outstanding work with IWBs, Tom recently worked closely with Philips to explore the possibilities of interactive technology in other forms, including the idea of an IWB table that students can sit around to interact in small groups.

Tom offered several snapshots into how he uses his IWB.

1   Positional language activity with Year 2 students:
We have a lovely outdoor nursery playground, which has lots of different areas for the children to enjoy, and I took a group of Year 2 children into it during a maths lesson to explore positional language. The children took photos of each other next to, standing on, in front of, behind all sorts of different furniture and objects that make up the playground. On returning to the classroom for the last part of the activity I uploaded the newly taken pictures to notebook pages I had prepared. They had a range of appropriate positional words that the children would be expected to use—a word bank that the children could choose from and add to their picture. In the second part of the lesson we worked as a small group on the IWB, annotating the pictures they had taken with the pens to highlight the different objects, as

well as using the word bank to label the pictures with the correct vocabulary. We used the combined experience of physically experiencing the positional concepts and the digital review that took place on the IWB to write some simple positional language sentences.

2   Transforming the teaching of handwriting:

Sometimes it is the on-tap functionality that an IWB brings into the classroom that can make a specific difference. The notebook recording feature of our IWBs has changed the way we support our children's handwriting practice in the classroom. Along with the usual tracing of the letter shapes—in the air, on their hands, on a partner's back—and the modelling of the joins we can now offer the children a replay of the letter joins in a short video clip. We use the IWB recorder software to save the modelled letter join and then play back the short film clip on loop. We then have the ability to step away from the IWB and not only do the children get an unobstructed view of the handwriting join, we can also work alongside them to support what they are doing. In this instance we are not tied to the IWB but use its functionality to allow us to step away and support the children at the point of writing. The children also find it very useful to be able to look up at any point and see the modelled example being played for them.

3   Roll call:

Use your IWB as a roll call in the morning for your class. This is a lovely idea to encourage the use of the IWB in Early Years classes—by the time the children start their lessons the whole class has already used the IWB at least once.

In your IWB notebook software create a 6x5 grid (for 30 students) that covers half of the page vertically. Add small headshot images of the children in the different boxes. Duplicate the grid on the opposite side of the page—if possible, duplicate the images as well, increase their transparency and lock them in place. These faint images will then act as placeholders for the other images on the left. When the children come into class, all they have to do is to find their picture and drag it across to the right-hand grid to show their attendance. It provides a nice focal point for the morning and every child present will use the board independently before the day kicks off.

For the children who are absent you could add little images or icons to show if they are on holiday (bucket and spade) or are unwell (thermometer).

At a glance, you can see who is present or absent. This idea works especially well for classes that have just got an interactive whiteboard or for Early Years children building their confidence in IWB skills.

4 Google Earth and the IWB: Where are we today?

Google Earth works really well with an IWB and this is an activity that I often start the day with. Choose a city and zoom down to street level so you can see a few square miles of the city. (Note: This is an example of what happened with my class on one of the first occasions we did this.) I then asked the children to guess where we were. I soon realised we could play a ten-question type game where they have only ten questions to guess the name of the city. It was great fun and soon the class were firing away with the questions.

Is it in the UK? Is it in Australia? Is it Athens?

Does the city have any famous buildings?

Wow! This last question blew me away for 9 am in the morning! So I answered, 'Yes, it has some very famous historic buildings you might know.' Well, it didn't take long for a couple of children to guess it was Rome.

I then zoomed out a little and switched on the 3D Buildings network link and we looked at the Colosseum. The children were enthralled as they used the IWB to pan and zoom into the ancient structure. We even navigated so we were standing on one of the terraces of the great amphitheatre. The 'wows' soon spread through the room—and there is nothing quite like starting the day with a good 'wow'!

We have to remember we are just looking at our planet, but it is Google Earth that allows us such easy and unique access to these wonders. The use of the IWB in this instance is unique as it allows the children the ability to manipulate a vast 3D environment with ease.

Tom regularly writes about his various classroom activities to share with others. You can read more on his blog at http://tbarrett.edublogs.org/.

KATIE MORROW—O'NEILL, USA

Katie Morrow teaches in the O'Neill Public Schools in Nebraska, where she has taught at both the elementary and high school levels although she currently works as a technology integration specialist for the district.

Highly involved in the Nebraska Educational Technology Association, she is an educator clearly passionate about the use of technology for learning, and in particular the use of SMART Board technology. Katie has received a number of recognitions for teaching excellence, including ISTE's national runner-up for Outstanding Teacher of the Year 2005 and Technology and Learning's Leader of the Year 2005. She is both a SMART Exemplary Educator and Apple Distinguished Educator, and her work with IWBs has been featured on the SMART Board Lesson podcast and the SMART Technologies Best Practices Case Study program.

Katie offers the following snapshot into her use of IWB technology.

By far one of the most engaging experiences for the students in my fifth grade classroom was creating our school news program entitled 'Eagle Eye News'. Each month students performed rotating jobs on the news team, including audio engineer, technical director, managing editor, camera crew, field reporter and anchor person, just to name a few. Each episode was entirely student produced—from writing the stories, through to filming and editing—and we utilised the SMART Board in every step of the process. Outlined below are a few of the ways our interactive whiteboard enhanced this rich language arts experience for my students and the wide audience with whom we shared our productions.

- *Prewriting: large group brainstorming and news story assignments*
- *Concept mapping (SMART Ideas or Inspiration) to plan each episode's 'flow'*
- *Editing and revising: peer editing and proofreading of word-processed stories*
- *Teleprompter: students scroll through the stories complete with colour-coded highlighters on the SMART Board during filming to make anchor people's eyes appear as if they are looking right into the camera*
- *Post-production: large group editing in iMovie*
- *Group critique: viewing each episode on the SMART Board in order to constructively critique it*
- *SMARTcasts: Students producing content with SMART Recorder*

In order for the SMART Board interactive whiteboard to be truly transformational in the educational process, it almost needs to become more transparent or invisible. By this I mean that instead of focusing on the flashiness and 'magic' of the IWB, we instead need to focus on the teaching and learning and use the technology as a vehicle, not a destination.

Sending our students into the twenty-first century as primarily passive receivers of information will not give them the skills needed to compete in an ever-changing global society Students of today thrive on being able to create, contribute and collaborate with the world around them. How, then, do we structure our classroom learning to encourage higher-level thinking skills and greater engagement in self-directed learning? Using the SMART Board for students to produce content, rather than just consume it, is a great first step.

The Recorder is a free tool included with SMART Board software. Students can create their lesson on any educational topic in SMART Notebook or any software application. After scripts are written and practising takes place, students start the Recorder tool while narrating the process and every action on the screen is recorded into the movie file. This simple way of turning our students into teachers can take on multiple formats, including all subject areas and even digital storytelling pieces of student interest. Extensions include scoring the movie with background music and posting to a web server to share with the world.

I have used the idea of SMARTcasts with my students as they created creative writing stories, math lessons for younger learners, and technology tutorials for their peers. Example SMARTcasts created by students can be viewed by following the links on my website.

Finally, I would love to share my resources involving SMART Board interactive whiteboards at: http://smartteach.wetpaint.com. Feel free to join the community, add to the discussion, or just download lessons and ideas to use in your own classroom.

Katie hosts her own website where she blogs, podcasts and shares her resources and ideas. You can find her online at http://www.mrs morrow.com.

LESLEIGH ALTMANN—KEMPSEY, AUSTRALIA

Lesleigh Altmann has had over 30 years experience teaching in metropolitan and country Catholic primary schools. She has taught all primary grades and held coordinator positions at St Joseph's Primary, Kempsey in New South Wales. She has been an IWB mentor for staff in primary schools under the Australian Government Quality Teaching Program and as a member of the Diocesan Interactivity Team for both Interactivity School Conferences in 2007 and 2008. Lesleigh now works as a mentor to teachers in the area of ICT support at St Joseph's Primary as well as at St Mary's in Bowraville, New South Wales. She was awarded a certificate of recognition by the Australian College of Educators for dedication and excellence in computing technology in 2004.

In our interview, Lesleigh described ways she uses IWBs and how she mentors other teachers to use them.

The introduction of the Interwrite technology into both primary schools [St Joseph's, Kempsey and St Mary's, Bowraville] brought about a mixed bag of responses among teachers. Some perceived such technology as beneficial and embraced its introduction with enthusiasm; others were more cautious in their approach to yet another skill to learn. My great interest is in mentoring and supporting both hesitant and enthusiastic teachers to use this exceptional interactive tool with confidence in order to create meaningful and engaging resources for their students.

There was the inevitable nose-dive during the implementation phase and we realised how important it was for teachers to have time to develop technical skills—with ongoing pedagogical support—to use the features of their Interwrite. I called this the 'IWB Implementation Dip' where the Interwrite was first used as a very expensive data projector. With a variety of formal, informal, collegial and professional mentoring programs, teachers began to experiment with Interwrite as an interactive tool for role modelling and joint construction before students engage in independent work.

Different approaches were employed by both schools in order to assist staff to meet these challenges. St Mary's developed a simple 'Scope and Sequence' for teachers to develop and practise Interwrite skills in a ten-minute timeslot. St Joseph's implemented a weekly mentoring program and after school 'Information Coffee and Learning Technology' sessions.

Try setting a similar 'Scope and Sequence' to suit yourself or a small group. Focus on a collaborative approach to develop sound skills in a graduated process for calibration, finding the devices, managing files correctly, exploring uses and features of various IWB tools, and then get back together next week and share your findings. Apply this method to gradually introduce teachers to an increasing number of tools, show them how to customise the toolbar and cruise around the Gallery together to become familiar with the images, backgrounds and sims. Hold sessions where teachers can work at the Interwrite together to build up a set of basic 'help documents' on the board as you go. This process offers the opportunity to learn more about the Interwrite and to share other essential computer skills.

Save these and keep them handy in a digital format or print them off and hang them beside the board. Having resources like this empowers every learner to be more independent!

I utilise the Interwrite's 'Record and Playback' feature to capture trouble-shooting methods or create lessons to email teachers as small video files.

And don't forget, your learning team includes the students. Get them involved!

Develop and share your ideas as a master file like the Interwrite Class List from St Joseph's Primary [Figure 8.1]. I worked with some teachers as a fun way to use the stamps to register swimming money, library books returned and home readers selected. Student pictures were cropped from a class group photo using the Capture tool and dragged across into the Interwrite Content Gallery. Shape tools and Line tools were employed to create a generic grid to create this page.

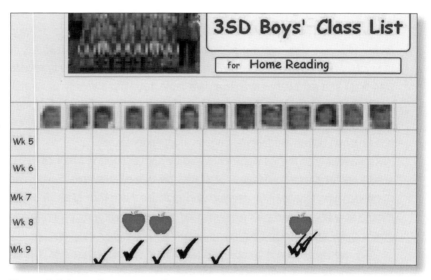

Figure 8.1 Interwrite class list, St Joseph's Primary

Another fabulous experience was to use Interwrite to demonstrate and model the techniques for constructing a podcast using Audacity. The Screen Capture tool came in very handy for capturing the steps into an Interwrite lesson file, which could be revisited by students later as they created podcasts like our Garraam Kids Podcast (http://www.bwpp.lism.catholic. edu.au) and for promotional advertisements that were played as part of the school phone system's 'on-hold' soundtrack.

I firmly believe that the key to successful IWB implementation is the acknowledgment of teachers' established ICT skills such as those developed in Microsoft Office, which can be used in combination with the IWBs. Use your established ICT or Microsoft Suite resources built up over previous years to adapt Interwrite technology so you can transform lessons into stimulating interactive activities. Start with these similarities to build up your confidence. Many of our staff have found it relatively easy to move from a known skill (in Microsoft Office) to an unknown environment (Interwrite).

At St Mary's, Bowraville, our Interwrite boards have been utilised in an ongoing process to change the way our students engage with the skill and enjoyment of reading and writing. We use the Interwrite Pen and Highlighter tools with our classes to address the deconstruction and reconstruction of text, and to connect information and make inferences on projected digital books [see Figures 8.2 and 8.3].

Use the Shape tool to create headings and then utilise the features of the Text tool to create text around the story to challenge student thinking.

Create sets of rectangles with the Shape tool. Move to the background with answers typed into the shapes with the Text tool. Then move this layer to the background to secure it. Create coloured rectangles and add questions to these shapes, and use the Grouping tool so the text stays on the shape when it is moved. This is a great strategy to stimulate discussion or create a memory game for any lesson [see Figure 8.4].

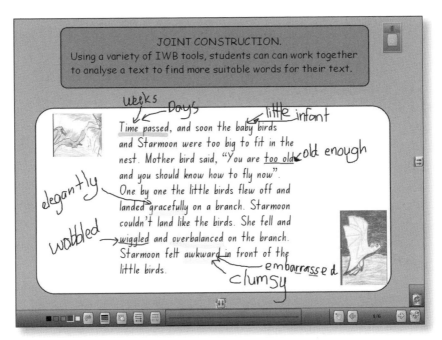

Figure 8.2 Using the Interwrite Pen and Highlighter tools (Example 1)

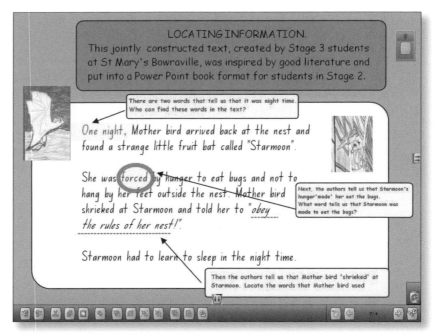

Figure 8.3 Using the Interwrite Pen and Highlighter tools (Example 2)

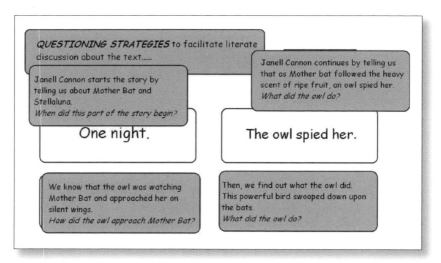

Figure 8.4 Creating rectangles to add questions and answers

St Mary's students wanted to create a class book to share with younger students. Research on fruit bats was conducted using the IWB's ability to hyperlink directly to the Internet and facts were collated on a Word document for the book. As part of the process, I created a research document that

was linked from the IWB lesson to an Internet site. Our students utilised the laptop rather than the on-screen keyboard for such a large amount of text. Pictures were drawn to support the text and scanned in JPEG format so they could be inserted into this Microsoft PowerPoint book template which the students called 'Starmoon' [see Figure 8.5].

Figure 8.5 Class book created by St Mary's students

The journey has begun. Using our existing Microsoft knowledge as a starting platform we are now beginning to infuse IWB technology across all subjects in order to move away from that initial stage of the IWB Implementation Dip. The Interwrite tools are now far less daunting. Good-quality work like this does not just happen without total immersion into good literacy programs, good use of IWB technology in the classroom and enthusiastic teachers.

KYLE STEVENS—DALLAS, USA

Kyle Stevens is a teacher/coach at Bishop Dunne Catholic School in Dallas, Texas. Kyle is in his ninth year of teaching and his sixth year at Bishop Dunne Catholic. He graduated with a Bachelor's degree in English and Political Science from the University of Kansas and is currently pursuing his Masters in Education from Regis University. Kyle teaches

English, world history and economics, and has been using IWBs for the past three years. He has also presented on effective uses of IWBs at local and regional conferences including the Geotech conference in Dallas and the Tech Forum Southwest in Austin, Texas, and was recently made an official SMART Exemplary Educator.

Kyle offers the following insights into his own IWB usage.

When considering the use of IWBs in education, people occasionally neglect the enormous benefits of this tool for the high school student, but the features that make the IWB a great tool for younger students can also be utilised at the high school level. In the three years I have been teaching with a SMART Board, I have found it to be beneficial in numerous ways, including the ability to conduct physically engaging discussions, to construct and organise ideas in ways that are visually appealing, and to focus the class on a specific area of the board. By using these tools, alongside the ability to export the Notebook pages, I have found an increase in student participation and understanding of the content.

As an English teacher, many of my lessons involve classroom discussions of literature. One such example is during our poetry unit. Each year my English class reads and analyses The Rose that Grew from Concrete *by Tupac Shakur. Using the SMART Board provides an opportunity for each student to share his or her thoughts and perspectives with the class as a whole. We begin our discussion with a single Notebook page containing solely the poem on it, and our discussion starts with an analysis of six different categories. By using the SMART Board, each member of the class can be engaged both in the verbal discussion as well as physically. The contribution of each student can be written on the board, either by the teacher or by the student. As our discussion progresses from an analysis of the title to a paraphrasing of the language used by the author, the colour displayed by the pen changes. This change in colour allows for the better organisation of the ideas expressed by the class.*

Another key feature of the SMART Board and the SMART Notebook used by my classes in the analysis of poetry is the Spotlight feature. The Spotlight allows me to focus the class on a single aspect of the poem. In poetry analysis it is common for the class to be overwhelmed, even in a short poem such as The Rose that Grew from Concrete. *In using the Spotlight, I can limit what the class sees. I can black out the majority of the poem and direct the class to individual lines. The class uses this feature when examining the poem for connotative devices present in the poem. As we dissect the poem, we again change the colour of the pen we use on*

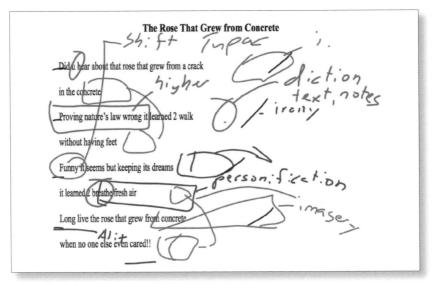

Figure 8.6 Using a SMART Board to analyse literature
(Courtesy: Amaru Entertainment/Estate of Tupac Shakur)

the SMART Board, so when concluded the class can visually recognise the repetition of connotative devices.

The final tool I rely upon when using the SMART Board is the ability to export the Notebook file into a PDF. This tool benefits both the students attending class as well as those absent from the discussion. While it is common for students to compare notes, equally important are the notes constructed by the teacher. Since I use this poem as a model for future poetry analysis, I constantly refer the students to our class discussion of this poem. By exporting the Notebook pages and uploading them to our online class page I am able to provide all students with these notes. This procedure is helpful since student notes can be incomplete or missing at the times they need them most.

The purpose of our class discussion is to model to students how they should analyse subsequent poems. While I have always used this poem in the initial class discussion, I have not always done so using a SMART Board. In the years prior to using a SMART Board I noticed that students had difficulty in isolating each stage of the analysis. In poetry analysis it is critical that students be able to focus on one stage at a time. By using the SMART Board, my classes have been able to enhance the analysis. As a high school teacher I feel that the use of the SMART Board is a highly effective tool with my students. My students use the engaging and visual learning activities to increase our ability to understand the information.

Kyle's class blog can be found at http://www.classblogmeister.com/blog.php?blogger_id=21053, while his personal reflections about education and technology are blogged at http://kstevens77.wordpress.com.

PAULA WHITE—VIRGINIA, USA

Paula White is a teaching veteran of 30-plus years who has won numerous awards for her use of technology in scaffolding student understanding and innovative uses of the web since 1991. She is currently a Gifted Resource teacher at Crozet Elementary School in the Albemarle County Public Schools System in Virginia. Paula is an Apple Distinguished Educator, a STAR Discovery Educator, a National Teacher Training Institute (NTTI) Master Teacher, a Phi Delta Kappa teacher of the year, and a ComputerWorlds Laureate. She has served on state and national conference committees as well as presented at conferences all over the US. Paula piloted the use of Airliners in her classroom for SMART Technologies and has presented on their use for two years at her state conference. Paula has worked with the National Gallery of Art in Washington, DC through their teacher institute for seven years promoting the use of digital storytelling and podcasting.

Paula's interest and expertise in Web 2.0 tools led the charge in her school system, and she has the following to say about her IWB.

> Students may like the 'interactivity' of IWBs, but the communal engagement of using them is the most powerful aspect. In too many cases teachers use IWBs to just fill in the blanks or answer closed questions on notebook activities, with the IWB simply being a big touch screen where kids compete to show they know the correct answer. Instead, as I plan, I search for ways that the technology changes the task or increases the depth of how the task is understood or completed. I also consider the potential for thoughtful conversations.
>
> Influential activities I use involve co-editing or co-creating a product to meet specific goals. Many teachers I work with use an 'Editor-in-Chief' method, where students read, edit and (sometimes) recopy in their best handwriting the edited text. When 'Editor-in-Chief' is done on the IWB, students observe peers modelling their thinking about the mistakes made and how to correct them. I often see an increase in intellectual risk taking as students become willing to share in order to have a turn to use the IWB. They actually clamour to edit!

Discussing student strategies and options for revision is also much easier than when students simply read their text aloud, describing what they did. The IWB allows for AND PROMOTES engagement through a variety of learning modes.

Another powerful activity involves teaching students summarising and note taking, a high-yield strategy identified by Robert Marzano. My students examine a text (we often use Wikipedia entries so we can explore issues of authenticity and accuracy) about a historical event, such as '... the importance of the American victory at Yorktown' (VA SOL Virginia Studies 5.c). We display the Siege of Yorktown Wikipedia text on the IWB, with two students using Airliner slates. The rest have their textbooks/laptops and history journals. I like the Airliners (a wireless slate connected to the display computer through Bluetooth technology) because students control the IWB from wherever they are in the room. Working from their seat puts the emphasis on the text on the IWB, not the person in front activating the board.

As everyone silently reads the text, they note vocabulary that may be an issue for or interesting to them. Students without Airliners attempt to condense the text into one sentence or main idea. Concurrently, one 'Airliner pilot' is using coloured pens to mark up the text on the IWB as the second pilot watches. The goal is to make learning and thinking transparent, and the use of the IWB facilitates this by allowing students to see what other students are doing, AS THEY ARE DOING IT. As students finish their independent work, they, too, watch the first pilot who is using the Airliner and IWB to make their thinking transparent.

We probe why Pilot 1 did what s/he did, and others naturally chime in to describe their process. When we have finished probing, we all contribute as Pilot 2 attempts the same two tasks (with more information and having had instruction), now synthesising and evaluating everything that has been said and done to this point. Doing this twice supports another of Marzano's strategies, reinforcing effort and providing recognition. Working, thinking, talking and learning together, we encourage each other to provide recognition for work well done, as we comment upon, agree or disagree and improve our understanding of essential content and effective summarising. The IWB is integral to this process of thinking and collaboration.

We then reflect upon condensing the entry into one sentence, discussing the efficiency, effectiveness and support for understanding that this provides. Marzano's research shows that students should substitute, delete and keep some things as they use the basic structure of the information presented. Using the IWB allows us, as a group, to work on the structure of the text, comparing and contrasting our first activity of a 'one sentence summary' to collaboratively creating a more effective summary.

When students share their processes and strategies, other students hear what they are looking at, paying attention to the connections they make as they read and work. Sharing this 'thinking about their thinking' provides models for less-experienced students to note that successful summarisers pay attention to things such as text features, the connections a reader makes (whether it be self to text, text to text, or text to world, etc.) and the vocabulary in the text so that they can use it or find synonyms as they restate the material in their own words.

Students learn to question what is unclear, seek clarification and analyse a text/topic to uncover what is central, restating it in their own words. Using the IWB to scaffold students observing, talking about and reflecting upon their own process supports deeper understanding. As we finish this lesson by collaboratively creating a clearly stated summary of our text, students show their noticeably increased understanding of summarising, and we all acknowledge that the IWB helped tremendously!

Paula maintains a blog with her personal thoughts about education at http://tzstchr.edublogs.org/, and a professional website at http://www.k12albemarle.org/Crozet—just follow the Gifted Resources link.

LOUISE GOOLD—SYDNEY, AUSTRALIA

Louise Goold is a Kindergarten teacher at Father John Therry (FJT) School, Balmain. Prior to becoming a teacher, Louise worked for many years as a speech pathologist supporting the speech, language and social development of children with additional needs. Her work as a communication consultant to metropolitan and rural schools and preschools convinced her to retrain as a teacher. Louise has only been teaching with an IWB for six months but loves the way it has transformed the learning experiences in her classroom. She also recently completed an online course in Web 2.0 and is full of ideas about its potential applications in the classroom.

In this snapshot, Louise shares the story of her 'Sallyboard'.

Receiving an interactive whiteboard in Term 2 of this year was a source of great excitement to all members of the Kindergarten class. The children insisted on naming the board 'Sally', the projector 'Zac', and our two pens 'Jill' and 'Bill'. Anthropomorphising this technology has generated a delightful sense of ownership and partnership within the classroom. As teacher and students we are co-learners, collaborators and conspirators in our journey of learning with 'Sally'.

I utilise the board constantly for enhancing my teaching of key learning areas, but I particularly like to use the board for reading and maths groups. There are many quality online learning experiences (if you are prepared to trawl!) that allow me to differentiate literacy and numeracy experiences to effectively meet the diverse learning needs within my classroom.

I can look at certain online activities as a whole class, explaining the outcomes of each experience—what the activity 'wants to help you learn', and then in small groups the children can either work at Sally independently, with the guidance of a parent helper or with me.

My top reading group can use Sallyboard to identify correct punctuation in a sentence. My emergent readers can use the board to identify beginning sounds and letters of words [see Figure 8.7].

Figure 8.7 Identifying sounds and letters using the IWB

I can make use of this appealingly noisy online hundreds chart to have my top maths group work with addition and subtraction with me: 'Show me what you get when you add four to seventy. Use the pattern of tens to take ten away from ninety.' I can use the same chart with different maths learners to get them to 'show me the number that comes after eleven' [Figure 8.8].

1	2	3	4	5	6	7	8	9	10
11	12	13	14	15	16	17	18	19	20
21	22	23	24	25	26	27	28	29	30
31	32	33	34	35	36	37	38	39	40
41	42	43	44	45	46	47	48	49	50
51	52	53	54	55	56	57	58	59	60
61	62	63	64	65	66	67	68	69	70
71	72	73	74	75	76	77	78	79	80
81	82	83	84	85	86	87	88	89	90
91	92	93	94	95	96	97	98	99	100

CLEAR

PRINT

MAIN

Figure 8.8 Fun with the hundreds chart
(http://www.primarygames.co.uk/pg2/splat/splatsq100.html)

In addition to making use of quality online resources, I can quickly generate meaningful teaching tools with Sally to support the acquisition of a particular concept. Take blending, for example: I can use Sally to model blending and have the children take turns blending without having to photocopy, laminate and locate large, colourful blends cards [Figure 8.9].

Figure 8.9 Group learning at the board

Sally also allows me to maximise teachable moments that I could not otherwise readily access resources for:

'Mrs Goold, what is breaching?'

'What an interesting question, Raef! Let's get a photo now from the Internet of whales breaching and investigate! Looking at the computer screen, what do I need to click on, to get onto the Internet? What does 'images' mean? What images will I ask Google to search for?' [Figure 8.10]

What does breaching look like?

jumping out of the water (Robert)
looks like it's leaping (Ruby)
not doing a bellyflop. doing a backflop (Raef)

Figure 8.10 Using images from the Internet to answer questions and extend the learning on the spot

As a Kindergarten teacher I love using my felt board to foster children's language and literacy development. It is one of many valued teaching tools I shall always use in the Infants classroom. Similarly, my interactive whiteboard has become another greatly valued classroom tool that I use, not only to foster language and literacy skills, but to develop and extend social skills, mathematical thinking, fine and gross motor skills, and cognitive skills such as attention, recall, convergent and divergent thinking ... and that's just ME! Imagine what it's doing for the children!

TOBIAS COOPER—SYDNEY, AUSTRALIA

Tobias Cooper teaches high school mathematics at Presbyterian Ladies College in Sydney. Tobias uses Promethean IWBs along with ActivStudio and a large collection of specialised mathematical software to teach his students maths in an engaging, interactive way. He also runs a successful maths teaching consultancy that focuses on assisting teachers with the use of IWB technology in the maths classroom.

Tobias offered the following comments about his IWB experience, which reflect the same pattern experienced by many other excellent IWB practitioners—one where initial doubts about the technology soon gave way to a rich use of interactivity to assist the visualisation of complex and abstract ideas, which conventional teaching technologies often struggle to do well.

> When I first saw IWBs in action I was a complete sceptic. I could not see how they could improve anything I was doing in the classroom. In hindsight, this view was formed because I had not seen a high school mathematics teacher use an IWB. I had only seen sales reps and primary school teachers use them. More importantly, I had never actually used an IWB myself before. My view on IWBs has changed significantly since I started using one on a daily basis.
>
> When I first started to use an IWB, one of the most powerful and simple uses I found for an IWB was the ability to directly interact with a wide range of images. Using screen capture software I could easily copy and paste any image into the IWB software and then annotate and write over it with different colours.
>
> For example, when teaching lessons on perimeter, I would copy and paste an image from the textbook on a CD and then calculate the length of each edge, using different coloured pens to highlight the edges as we go around the shape. This surprisingly simple technique allows the students to visually see what lengths have been determined and which lengths have not [see Figure 8.11].
>
> Demonstrating the formula for calculating the area of a triangle using an IWB is also a simple yet powerful experience for students. Using the Rectangle and Polygon tools, I would create the diagram shown on page 125 [Figure 8.12]. The Fill tool is then used to fill the region's exterior to the triangle.

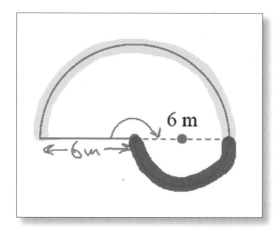

Figure 8.11 Using coloured pens as a visual tool in maths

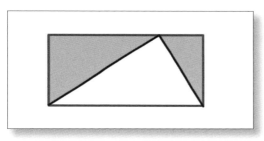

Figure 8.12 Using visual tools to calculate the area of a triangle (Example 1)

The shaded regions are then selected, rotated, moved and manipulated into position inside the triangle, clearly demonstrating that the area inside the triangle is exactly the same as the area outside the triangle [Figure 8.13]. Simple manipulations such as this make it much easier for students to understand that the area of the rectangle is twice the area of the triangle, and leads to a very concrete example of the formula Area = ¹/₂ (base x height).

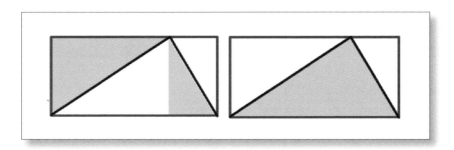

Figure 8.13 Using visual tools to calculate the area of a triangle (Example 2)

IWBs have also helped to overcome many practical difficulties associated with geometric constructions. For example, bisecting an angle with a traditional blackboard or whiteboard compass was always prone to mistakes because the compass kept slipping on the board. However, the virtual compass on an IWB makes this activity mistake free, accurate and a whole lot more fun [Figure 8.14].

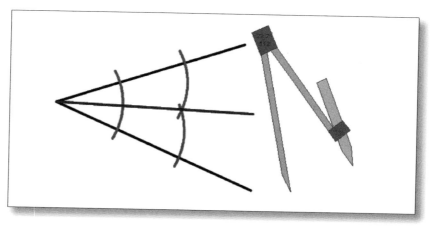

Figure 8.14 Using the virtual compass on the IWB

The ability to move and manipulate virtual objects on an IWB is clearly one of the most powerful features available to teachers and students. For example, a class can be set a series of patterns to build using real matchsticks. After the activity, the teacher can ask students to come and demonstrate their solution on the IWB using virtual matchsticks. For example, in the puzzle below [Figure 8.15], the students have to remove four matches to make

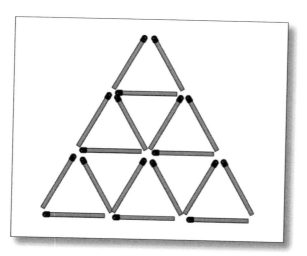

Figure 8.15
Manipulating matchsticks on the IWB as part of a problem-solving task

six triangles. If the student makes a mistake or wants to start again, the reset button can be used to easily reset the pattern so that the student can try the problem again.

The educational possibilities for other software are also enhanced by an IWB. For example, writing the answers on a test or worksheet can be done electronically on an IWB. Going through test questions with the class is now seamless because the teacher can display the same questions as on the students' test or worksheet. The results can be saved for future reference and sent to absent students via email or posted on the school's website for downloading.

Geometry and graphing software are given more capabilities with an IWB. For example, a geometry program called GeoGebra allows the user to drag any geometrical object and see its algebraic representation change dynamically. This allows a student to drag geometrical objects on the IWB and discuss the results.

CHAPTER **9**

PROFESSIONAL DEVELOPMENT, TRAINING AND SUPPORT

In most schools there are usually one or two teachers who manage to almost instantly see the potential of new technology. We all know the type—for them, using technology seems as natural as breathing air. When they turn up for a staff training session they end up teaching the trainer things they didn't know. It is still unclear exactly why some people pick up technology so quickly, while others need various degrees of training and support before they feel any comfort in using it. These people are wonderful resources in a school, and if you happen to have one of them on staff you should consider yourself fortunate.

However, while it may be good to have one of these techno-gurus on staff, the key to creating a truly successful technology integration program is not how clever the technologists can be, but rather how well the school manages the ongoing training and support needed to help every teacher move forward in their use of technology. When every teacher in the school reaches an acceptable level of proficiency, only then can everyone claim to be moving towards a successful implementation of technology for learning.

Ideally, development and support in the use of technology— starting with the use of IWBs, but eventually extending to other areas of technology integration—need to be woven into the everyday operations of the school so that it just seems so normal that no one thinks of doing otherwise. This vision could well seem an almost unattainable goal in those schools that only get a few PD days every year, but it ought to be the goal, nonetheless. With new digital technologies seeming to appear each week, and constantly updated versions of software and Web 2.0

tools being released in an almost relentless stream, it has become more important than ever that all teachers are exposed to the possibilities and opportunities of how these new tools might be used in their teaching.

The other thing teachers will find as their digital literacy grows is that their expectations, and indeed those of their students, will continue to grow as they become more competent and confident in the use of their IWB and its associated digital technologies. As suggested in earlier chapters, initially they will probably use the tools to better do what they have always done, but within months new possibilities will emerge. As more and more of the teaching staff at the school start to embrace the possibilities of a digitally rich learning environment, their enthusiasm, knowledge and appreciation of what can be done with them will also grow and develop a critical mass.

MAKING IT SCHOOL-BASED

Ideally, the majority of professional development in ICT, including interactive whiteboards, ought to occur within the school as a regular part of a staff member's school life. It is important to offer regular PD opportunities to staff, which could take a wide variety of forms, ranging from organised after-school workshops, to lunchtime show-and-tell sessions, to peer mentoring, to a regular five-minute share session at staff meetings. Exactly how these ICT PD sessions are squeezed into the program will depend largely on the way the school is organised, but it is important that it does happen in some form.

There is a general belief among many leading educational thinkers that the time for schools to respond to the technology-driven cultural shift taking place in society is right now, and that education systems that fail to adapt and respond to these shifts now could find themselves becoming dangerously irrelevant. Some have suggested that the year 2014 will be somewhat of a tipping point. Schools that have not adopted a sense of urgency in making this shift over the next few years will face a big struggle in maintaining relevance to their students. If your school's staff training programs in ICT have been sloppy or half-hearted or relatively ineffective up until this point, now is the time to take a more focused approach.

Whether your school is an 'IWB school' or not, the issue of embedding technology-rich activities into your curriculum, is something that will become more and more critical over the next few years. Marc Prensky's

(2007) 'digital immigrants/digital natives' metaphor, although greatly over-simplified, is a useful starting point for understanding the characteristics of the millennial generation and why our traditional view of schooling no longer works so well for these students, the great bulk of whom will be passing through our schools in the next few years.

Think about the ICT PD that has been offered since computers appeared in schools back in the 1980s. Many school systems have collectively spent millions of dollars over the last 20-plus years trying to encourage teachers to learn and use technology better, but that support has often been provided in a way that stops short of actually mandating its use. As we approach the end of the first decade of the twenty-first century there now needs to be a sense of urgency about not only getting teachers up to speed with ICT but in ensuring that it is used in regular, effective and pedagogically sound ways with students.

As far as possible, your school should aim to provide the majority of the staff with in-house ICT PD. By all means, look to using external training, school visits and conferences as supplementary to the everyday support within the school, but providing in-house training and support allows it to be tailored for each member of the teaching team. In-house training also provides greater flexibility for just-in-time learning so that teachers can get what they need, as they need it. This aspect is particularly important for ICT- and IWB-related learning.

While you might be working in an educational authority that provides training at a central location, history has consistently shown that off-site training will only ever be used by a small proportion of the teachers in your school. You want everyone involved, all the time. Use the external training, organise visits to schools that are doing great things and get money set aside to send groups of teachers off to the best conferences. But use all these things to supplement your in-school PD activities, not replace them.

NATURE OF THE TRAINING AND SUPPORT

In considering the best form of training and support for your school's situation, do not lose sight of the immense amount of professional expertise that exists in the school's current group of teachers. After all, this is about teaching first and foremost, and all staff members have particular expertise that they can contribute to the overall picture—expertise that has nothing whatsoever to do with technology. All schools will have teachers who have individual strengths in areas like reading, choral work, communications, maths, science, information literacy, art, computer graphics, multimedia … the list goes on and on. Aim to factor the use of this diverse expertise into your professional development model, bringing together the ICT training and the curriculum expertise at every opportunity. Staff who are beginning to embed ICT into their teaching need to be assured that its main purpose is to enhance the excellent work they already do, and not to diminish the quality teaching currently taking place in their classrooms.

The nature of the training and support model your school chooses will range along a continuum, from training in specific technical competences ('How do I use the camera tool on the IWB?'), all the way through to how best to use a teacher's new-found skills in teaching particular areas of the curriculum ('How can I use existing multimedia and IWB tools to help me build better, more meaningful lessons?'), and beyond that, to extend into the development of quality teaching materials ('How can I tap into the broader digital world beyond the classroom to build more relevant and engaging teaching resources that are useful to me and my colleagues?'). Indeed, at the latter end it will be hard to decide whether it is teacher support or curriculum development.

In the initial phase of IWB use it will be important to assist all teachers to become proficient in the use of the technology, and in particular the specific 'flipbook' teaching software being used with your school's brand of boards. During this period, the most valuable resources needed to develop these key competencies will be time and support.

The great thing with IWBs is that the acquisition of those competencies can be phased, and their use graduated from the basic to highly advanced. That said, IWB tools are designed to make it simple for teachers to be creating professional-looking, interactive multimedia teaching materials. Start simple, but keep moving along that continuum.

THE VALUE OF MENTORING

Some schools have the added luxury of a full-time technology support person whose role it is to assist teachers integrate technology across the curriculum. One of the big advantages of such a support person is the way they are able to look at the teaching taking place in classrooms and find ways to support and extend that learning with a more technology-rich approach. Not all schools are in this position, of course, although a growing number of schools across all sectors are realising the need for a technology support role. Many schools do assign someone to that role, even if it is created with a part-time release from other teaching duties. It is good to have someone to turn to.

However, as good as it may be to have an ICT guru to call upon, eventually it will become apparent that to maintain ongoing ICT support over the years it makes more sense to develop a team of teachers with a range of expertise that staff can call upon for assistance in specific areas. This team can provide assistance with ideas for ways to teach a particular concept or for help in preparing digital teaching materials.

There are a number of problems with having a single ICT expert on staff, partly to do with the 'all your eggs in one basket' issues that arise when that person eventually moves on, but mainly in the undesirable message it sends to the rest of the staff. Having a single expert on staff leads people to start believing that ICT is hard, that you have to be an expert, that it is not for mere mortals, and that they have to be somehow gifted to use technology well. Be careful of this! One particular school brought in a group of highly competent outside experts to train staff in how to use the IWBs, and although the training was excellent, it created the mistaken belief in many staff members that to use an IWB well required some special ability. Consequently, many teachers at this particular school were very slow to truly embrace IWB technology because the bar had been set so high. Training has to be good, but it also has to be real and able to be duplicated by everyone else.

A team of mentors working within the school creates a much more authentic environment for learning, with new teaching ideas rapidly flowing through to other members of staff. Having a team of mentors, all with an appropriate teaching allowance to give them time to share, means it can more readily be refreshed when a key member or two moves on.

Bear in mind when creating your mentoring teams to incorporate any existing support structures. Many schools will already have a strong school library or information services team. Involve them in the support and development model.

While most of the day-to-day training and support can be integrated into the school's operations, there is much to be said for the occasional whole-staff event where there is the chance to hear what others are doing or to learn of their concerns. This sharing works particularly well if schools can organise these gatherings across their whole education authority, or at least across other schools in the same sector or area, and when they are focused on looking not only at IWBs but digital teaching generally. This practice not only serves to enhance a greater sense of community and learning; it also provides a great insight into the state of play beyond just your own school.

TIME

Ask any teacher to take on extra training and the answer will nearly always be: 'I don't have time.' Without doubt, teaching is an incredibly busy profession with a multitude of demands both in and out of the classroom. Sure, technology may be important, but so are the many other things that fill a teacher's busy day.

It ought to be obvious that the most important factor for success of any training or support program is time. Teachers need time to learn new technology; they need time to experiment with new tools, to become competent in their use and to work with colleagues to produce new and exciting teaching materials; they need time to play in the sandpit; they need time to reflect on how to use technology better.

That time usually costs money. Finding the time will usually come in the form of releasing teachers from other duties, which may include face-to-face teaching, playground duty or other such demands. The task is to convince the school and/or education authority leadership of schools to provide teachers with a pool of release time that can be drawn upon when required.

How much time your school will require is very difficult to say, as each situation will differ. Similarly, the points at which the school will need to call upon that time will vary. Suffice to say that school leaders need to be willing to set aside significant blocks of time for teacher release. This release time is not a luxury but a legitimate requirement for teachers trying to keep up with a world that is changing faster than ever before.

Some of this much-needed time can be reclaimed by re-prioritising the way existing time is spent. Take staff meetings, for example. Many schools have very successfully used their traditional staff meeting time for 'show-and-tell' sessions and staff reflection on the best uses of their IWBs. A number of the pathfinding schools have allocated every second week's 'admin' meeting for sharing ideas on how best to use the technology, calling upon the various teaching teams and specialists to show their work on the boards to other teachers on their staff. Time usually taken at staff meetings for administration matters—such as notices about upcoming events, etc.—can be used far more efficiently using email, so that precious face-to-face time could be given over to sharing and encouraging professional conversations about teaching.

Another possibility might be to schedule regular sharing sessions in times when teachers can get together. For primary school teachers, it could be when the students are with other specialist teachers for music, art or library; for high school teachers, it could be when they are off-class so they can use this time to get together with other teachers who are off-class. Ideally this can be done with others who teach the same grade level or subject, but this is not critical. Usually teachers will need to work within the constraints of their timetables. The important thing is that regular time is being allocated to sharing ideas and tips for using the IWBs (or other ICT resources).

Some schools have developed student mentor programs, where teams of selected students are trained on how to use the IWBs and then used as a resource for assisting teachers. Students will often pick up the use of technology very quickly, and although they will not be thinking about the use of the IWBs from a pedagogical perspective, they can be a great resource for teachers who are still getting used to the boards. Teachers bring their teaching expertise and partner with students who bring their technical expertise. Combining teacher-smarts with student-smarts can be a wonderfully empowering and liberating experience for both parties.

The critical step in getting ongoing professional development to happen is to just do it. Like so many other parts of life, getting good at using your interactive whiteboards relies on taking action and just doing it. Use them regularly and find ways to share stories about that use.

FINANCING

Time is money. If teachers are to have time to develop professionally, then money must be allocated for the vital task of ongoing development and support. Exactly how much will depend on the individual situation and the degree of control the principal has over the school's funding and deployment of staff. But for the program to succeed, money must be found. As always, the leadership will be the difference between a great IWB program and one that limps along on life support.

The school executive must make a commitment to the successful, ongoing use of the IWBs and the associated digital tools by everyone, and will need to ensure that things are appropriately funded. To get a better idea of what to expect, the executive should discuss with similar schools using IWBs how much they have set aside each year. Part of the major costs will be in staff salaries, funds to cover the cost of relief or back-up teachers, and funds to cover the annual cost of the teacher mentors. There will be a concentrated spending over the first year or two and then less will probably be required, but providing the funds to get the program off the ground over those first few years will be a make or break decision. Once the school develops a critical mass of IWB expertise, less will be required to keep it going—although funding will still be needed to cover new teachers joining the school.

One factor that does have an amplifying effect on both funding and PD needs is for schools to have a clear policy about the ICT skills of new staff before they enter the system. If the school has made a commitment to providing a technology-rich learning environment, then there ought to be clear expectations during the interview process that technology skills are important criteria for employment. Many schools are still hiring staff with surprisingly low levels of technology skill, and then needing to find significant funding to get them up to speed. It is amazing to hear of schools that claim to be committed to IWBs and ICT but who do not ask potential new staff about their use of these. Imagine the effect if every new staff member in your school did not need to start with basic training, but instead came on board with a good range of new ICT skills that they could use and share with others.

Of course, this is not to say that a person's technology skills should be the only criterion for employment, but if a school has made a serious educational and financial commitment to IWBs, and ICT in general, then employing staff who already have many of the desired skills is not an unreasonable expectation. It is appreciated that not all school systems have the authority to make such decisions, and some may have many other educational priorities besides technology, but for those that do claim technology as an important part of their educational culture, a raised level of expectation about technology skills for all new staff is something worth considering.

Beyond this, schools need to have money allocated for staff to attend workshops or to engage the services of specialist trainers, and—most importantly—for sending teaching teams to attend appropriate local or national conferences. There are a growing number of major IWB conferences that bring together hundreds of IWB practitioners to share ideas and techniques. Some of the best implementation success stories have started with a core group of teachers who all attended an IWB conference event together and then used the momentum from that event to launch the school forward in their IWB usage, taking many of their colleagues along in the slipstream of their new enthusiasm. A large part of the success of such stories revolves around getting a group to attend the conference, not just one or two teachers. One very successful IWB school even takes out loans with the church development fund to ensure teams of key staff are rewarded each year with a trip to their national IWB conference.

Finally, don't forget that when those staff members return from a conference event there needs to be planned opportunities for them to share what they experienced, as well as initial agreement from attendees that such sharing is part of the deal of going in the first place. This post-event sharing enables them to pass on many of the great ideas and tips they will have picked up, together with some of their enthusiasm and renewed vision, making sure that the money invested into the few has the best possible chance of having some impact upon the many.

MAINTAINING AN EDUCATIONAL FOCUS

In all the planning for the provision of appropriate training and support, we must keep in mind that its prime purpose is ultimately to enhance student performance. We all know how easy it is to get swept along by new technology, but as professionals we need to remember that we are simply using it to assist in providing quality teaching. We must stay focused—we don't teach technology, we teach students.

If your education authority or government has specified the key outcomes on which the school's performance will be measured (rightly or wrongly), your challenge will be to develop a training and support model that ultimately enhances the designated attributes.

In using the new technology it is very easy to get carried away with the many exciting things that can be done and to forget that the technology is nothing but a tool intended to assist the desired student learning. In the UK, for example, the decision to implement IWBs in the early 2000s was based on an intention to improve student literacy and numeracy nationally. Higgins and his team in their longitudinal study (Higgins, 2005) of the use of the boards for that purpose noted that one of the major shortcomings was that many of the schools involved failed to focus the teacher training on improving literacy and numeracy; instead, the focus was on how to use the technology. Do not get the baby mixed up with the bathwater!

Related to this is the importance of integrating the use of the boards into the existing school programs. Many seem to fall into the trap of placing the focus on the boards themselves and to quickly forget once again that they are only tools, like the humble blackboard, to assist the teachers in working through their programs. While IWBs are potentially many times more powerful than the blackboard, and experience indicates they do allow teachers to move faster than before through their programs, they are simply there to support the provision of quality teaching and learning.

THE REAL CHALLENGE

Although everything you have just read about training and support will probably seem blindingly obvious, history shows that the vast majority of governments, education authorities and schools across the developed world spend a lot more time talking about providing appropriate technology support than actually delivering it. Too often the specific needs of teachers are poorly targeted and most PD programs fail to adequately assist teachers to get what they need, when they need it.

Unless professional development can be structured in an ongoing, relevant and on-demand way, experience suggests that much of it will be wasted. Although it can be a huge challenge, getting the focus on a whole-school approach to ongoing PD will make a major difference to your progress with ICT.

GRASSROOTS PROFESSIONAL DEVELOPMENT

The participatory nature of the read/write web has enabled another, less traditional, style of professional development. Web 2.0, with its vast online global communities, has become a fertile ground for educators looking for others to share and collaborate with. As teachers connect with other teachers, large networks of like-minded individuals are forming online. Within these networks, educators are sharing, talking, learning and collaborating together like never before possible.

These networks of people all helping each other to learn—now usually referred to as Personal Learning Networks or PLNs—are reshaping the way many educators view professional development. Instead of waiting for their school to deliver professional development and training, these PLNs are creating a global learning environment for many educators that operates all year, working across schools, educational sectors, countries and time zones. Armed with tools like blogs, wikis, podcasts and instant messaging, these educators are refusing to wait for the system to provide PD and are mobilising themselves to learn from their peers whenever and however they need it.

This chapter will conclude with a couple of brief snapshots into the way some of these tools are being used to redefine what professional development means in the twenty-first century.

'Thirty-eight [and counting] Interesting Ways to Use Your Interactive Whiteboard'

GoogleDocs is Google's collection of free, online productivity tools. The GoogleDocs suite offers a word processor, spreadsheet and presentation tool that work very much like most other commercial productivity offerings, with one big difference: the files created by these applications are not saved on our computers' local hard drive, but instead reside on Google's servers on the Internet. Because they are stored 'in the cloud', documents created with GoogleDocs can be accessed from anywhere and by anyone with permission to do so.

UK teacher Tom Barrett, who was mentioned in Chapter 8 as having an interest in the use of GoogleDocs with his students, decided to use this characteristic of anywhere, any time accessibility to create a PowerPoint-like presentation for other teachers called 'Ten Interesting Ways to Use Your Interactive Whiteboard'. After creating the first few slides, Tom then threw the presentation open to anyone who wanted to contribute to it, hence the fact that currently (that is, at the time of writing) the presentation is called 'Thirty-eight Interesting Ways to Use Your Interactive Whiteboard'. As other teachers keep adding new ideas to this presentation, Tom keeps updating the title to reflect the current number of slides. Contributors to the slideshow have come from all over the world. These other educators simply email Tom to ask for permission to edit the document and then go ahead and add their idea on a new slide. It is a wonderful example not only of collaboration, but also of how educators around the world are taking it upon themselves to create their own professional development. By sharing with each other, they are all learning from each other.

You can visit Tom's presentation (and even add the next tip number if you wish) at http://docs.google.com/Presentation?docid=dhn2vcv5_106c9 fm8j&hl=en_GB.

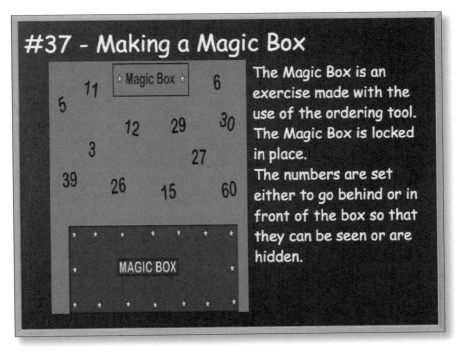

Figure 9.1 Tip number 37 of 'Interesting Ways to Use Your Interactive Whiteboard' (Courtesy: Tom Barrett)

The Interactive Whiteboard Challenge

Jess McCulloch (also mentioned in Chapter 8) is the brains behind the Interactive Whiteboard Challenge. Not content with sharing her passion for IWBs with only those in her immediate geographical area, Jess decided to use a wiki to create a website where people could register to accept her Interactive Whiteboard Challenge.

First, she contacted people whom she knew were highly experienced in the use of IWBs—people like Tom Barrett, Danny Nicholson, Ben Hazzard and others. She then asked these 'Task Masters' to each contribute a challenge—a specific IWB task or activity that would cause the participants to get to know their interactive board and software much better. The tasks were open-ended enough that any brand of IWB could be used, and most of the challenges were presented by the Task Masters using online video so that participants could see exactly what they needed to do. Once a participant rose to one of the challenges and completed it with their own IWB in their own classroom, they were then encouraged to blog about it, listing their blog URL on the wiki so that others could read about their experiences.

This simple concept is a perfect example of how the tools of Web 2.0 are being used to redefine what professional development is all about, effortlessly crossing the boundaries of place and time and enabling sharing on a massive global scale. You can read more about it, and take the Interactive Whiteboard Challenge yourself, at http://whiteboardchallenge. wikispaces.com/.

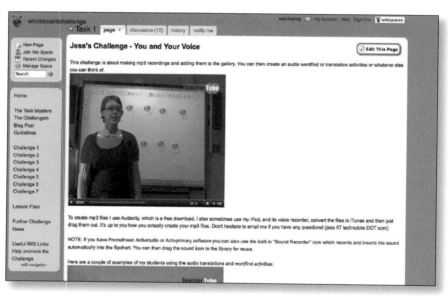

Figure 9.2 Jess McCulloch's Interactive Whiteboard Challenge
(Courtesy: Jess McCulloch)

OzNZ Educators

Not content to sit around waiting for professional development opportunities, Australian teacher Sue Tapp took it upon herself to start a regular weekly conversation with other educators interested in talking about the use of technology in their classrooms. Using a freely available online chat tool called FlashMeeting (http://flashmeeting.e2bn.net), Sue started scheduling regular Sunday evening get-togethers for anyone who wanted to join in. She called the group the OzNZ Educators group, since it was mainly Australians and New Zealanders who were around at that time on a Sunday night, but the sessions get regular visits from educators in Europe, Asia and the Americas.

The FlashMeeting tool supports text, audio and video, so attendees to Sue's meetings will generally use their computer's webcam and microphone to talk 'face to face' with their colleagues, most of whom they have never met in person. Conversation is partly social but mostly professional, with much discussion about what everyone is doing in their schools with technology. As a learning experience these sessions provide a great opportunity for teachers to tap into the wisdom of others while sharing ideas about best practice, handy tips for using technology and some inspirational stories about what goes on in other classrooms. Sue's FlashMeeting sessions can hold up to 25 participants and are recorded so they can be played back for later review. For more information about the OzNZ Educators group, including a weekly agenda, take a look at http://edhouse.wikispaces.com/Meeting+topics.

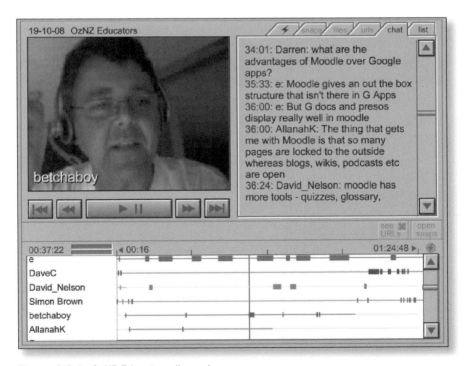

Figure 9.3 An OzNZ Educators discussion

(Courtesy: Sue Tapp)

Sue has also extended the community of educators that has grown around the Sunday night FlashMeetings by creating another sharing space using Ning, a managed social networking tool (http://oznzeducators. ning.com), as well as a group for sharing resources on the social book-marking site Diigo (http://groups.diigo.com/groups/oz-educators). Sue's work is a great example of what can be achieved when the tools of the social web are put to use to mobilise and self-organise people with a common interest in learning.

The SMARTBoard Lessons Podcast

Canadian educators Ben Hazzard and Joan Badger have spent the past three years recording a weekly podcast for teachers, called the SMART-Board Lessons Podcast. Filled with tons of useful tips, their podcast generally follows a successful format that includes segments like 'Links You Can Use', 'Blog Love', a useful lesson each week that looks at different ways of using an IWB, and a regular guest spot where teachers from all over the world drop in for a chat. The back-and-forth banter between Ben and Joan makes them great fun to listen to and they manage to turn technology professional development into a thoroughly entertaining experience.

Figure 9.4 SMARTBoard Lessons Podcast
(Courtesy: Ben Hazzard and Joan Badger)

Although the podcast focuses mainly on the use of SMART Boards, the ideas it contains are applicable to just about any brand of board. Being experienced educators, Ben and Joan are always bringing the lessons back to the underlying pedagogical basics, so it is never just about technology for technology's sake but rather about building on sound teaching concepts and discussing how learning can be made more effective with the wise use of interactive technology.

At the time of writing, the podcast had just recorded its 150th (and final) episode, but the archive of past podcasts is still available for download. You can browse the entire back catalogue of Ben and Joan's work at http://www.pdtogo.com/smart.

The K12 Online Conference

Our final example shows how effectively professional development can be driven by a grassroots approach. It is a wonderful demonstration of how networks of people can self-mobilise to learn together on a global scale.

In 2006, three teachers—two from the US and one from Canada—had an idea for using the web to connect educators from around the planet and transform the way they experience professional development. Wes Fryer, Sheryl Nussbaum-Beach and Darren Kuropatwa had a vision for a global, online conference in which the presentations, workshops and discussions were all created as digital media files, podcasts or vidcasts. An American teacher, Lani Ritter-Hall, assisted them for the 2007 event. In 2008, Ritter-Hall stepped down and Canadian educator Dean Shareski stepped into her shoes.

The core idea behind the conference is that teachers from all around the world freely share their expertise with their colleagues, who are able to watch or listen to these presentations and then engage in conversation through blogs, chats and live events. In October 2006, over a three-week period, the first K12 Online Conference was launched with a smorgasbord of over 40 digital presentations, four different live events and an explosion of online conversation about learning with technology. In this first year, the conference website attracted over 110 000 hits.

Since then, K12 Online has generated a further 80-plus digital presentations during 2007 and 2008, and connected thousands of educators from all over the world in conversations about teaching and learning. Since its inception in 2006, the site has had almost 320 000 hits from over 130 countries. Most traditional 'real' conferences cannot compete with the global reach of this model of professional development.

Figure 9.5 The K12 Online Conference
(Courtesy: K12 Online Convenors)

Since the beginning, all the presentations and dialogue have been archived online so it is, in effect, a conference that never ends. You can go back and browse through the K12 Online library of professional development resources any time you like, making it possible to learn what you need, when you need it.

OVER TO YOU!

Thanks to podcasts, wikis, GoogleDocs, live video chats and other tools like Twitter, Ning, VoiceThread, Second Life and Wordpress, professional development is no longer restricted to the one or two PD days each year that most schools can offer. A motivated teacher who is eager to learn more can now tap into targeted professional development at any time or place, in whatever way they choose to learn. There is no need to wait until someone can 'train you'. Building your own Personal Learning Network, and using the tools and people that best fit your own learning needs, is the perfect answer to the on-demand, ongoing nature of effective PD.

The answers you need, and the communities that can help you, are all out there just waiting for you to join the conversation.

CHAPTER **10**

MOVING FORWARD

Once it gets all the teachers using interactive whiteboards, probably the greatest challenge for your school will be to consistently sustain and enhance the use of the technology. Schools have historically demonstrated a marked propensity, particularly when key staff members move on, to revert back to old ways.

The goal—and the challenge—for you and your colleagues is to embed the use of IWBs and the associated digital technologies into the everyday operations of the school, and to have them become such a normal part of everyday teaching and learning that people basically forget about them. Few people give much thought these days to the use of the pen, the book or the teaching board, yet these were all considered new technologies for learning at one point. When your use of IWB technology has become so embedded that you reach this same level of transparency, you will know you are on your way to real success.

Related to this is the challenge of getting every member of staff to use their IWB as a digital hub to consistently enrich the effectiveness of learning and efficiency of their teaching. It is one thing to get a handful of teachers using IWBs and their associated digital toolkit, but it is quite another to have the entire teaching staff become expert in their use. And yet, this is when the real magic starts to happen; not because of the use of technology per se, but because of the cultural and educational shifts that go along with such a situation. When the entire teaching staff within a school embraces the pedagogical changes required to provide an engaging and digitally rich environment in which to learn, the shift can scarcely be avoided.

We have talked about the fact that many new IWB users start out by using the boards to do many of the same traditional teaching tasks they have always done. It is what one would expect of early or novice users.

As teachers move along the continuum of teaching with an IWB, however, they need to be harnessing the immense potential of the technology to explore entirely new ways of enriching the learning.

Remember that to achieve this ongoing development, you will need to simultaneously address a set of key variables. The importance of the school principal in visioning, leading and funding this ongoing development cannot be overstated. As in so many areas of life, everything rises and falls on leadership. Beyond this, however, remember that there are a number of other school-wide developments that must be part of the cultural shift to e-teaching. Many of these things have already been discussed in detail elsewhere in this book, but they include such things as:

- standardisation on IWB hardware and software that meets the pedagogical needs of the learners
- a well thought-out and communicated plan and implementation strategy
- a reliable and robust ICT infrastructure designed primarily to support the tasks of teaching and learning
- an effective whole-staff professional developmental program
- inclusion of students in the planning and mentoring process
- just-in-time ICT support that focuses on curriculum as the central component, not technology
- strategies in place to share and enrich the teaching of all members of staff
- regular celebration of the successes being made by learners, teachers and the school
- regular reflection and evaluation of the entire process.

The ability to coordinate and authorise all these interdependent factors rests with a number of key groups within the school: the principal, department heads, technical support staff, parents, students, and of course teachers. For an effective implementation of IWBs, all these key groups need to work with each other and support the overall goals of enriching learning for the students. Ultimately, though, the responsibility for what actually happens in the classrooms rests with the individual classroom teachers, not just the leadership. To a very large degree, it is up to every teacher to be an educational leader, even if only in some small way.

THE BIG PICTURE IS WHAT MATTERS

The international research on interactive whiteboards consistently reiterates that the most important variable in improving student learning is the quality of the teaching that takes place within the school. Although this book has tried to focus on some of the technical, pedagogical and logistical issues of implementing IWBs successfully, the point remains that none of this matters if these are not being applied on top of quality teaching practice. It bears saying once more that an excellent teacher with limited resources will nearly always be able to provide a better learning experience than an inferior teacher who has all the latest technology. Technology, in and of itself, is not the answer to more effective learning. Good-quality teaching by passionate, committed educators is the answer to more effective learning. It always has been, and always will be.

An IWB is nothing but a tool to assist great teachers in doing what they do best. All the high praise or damning criticism you might hear about IWB technology is largely irrelevant without an insight into how a teacher is using this tool. An IWB can be used as a regular dry-erase whiteboard, a basic electronic whiteboard or a dynamic digital convergence facility that sits at the centre of a media-rich digital teaching hub. It is the teacher, not the technology, that decides how effectively an IWB will be used in their classroom.

Good luck with your IWB journey!

BIBLIOGRAPHY

Balanskat, A., Blamire, R., & Kefala, S. (2006, December 11). *The ICT impact report: A review of ICT impact on Schools in Europe.* Retrieved July 16, 2008, from http://ec.europa.eu/education/doc/reports/doc/ict impact.pdf.

Barber, M., & Mourshed, M. (2007). *How the world's best performing school systems come out on top.* McKinsey & Company. Retrieved July 16, 2008, from http://www.mckinsey.com/clientservice/socialsector/resources/pdf/Worlds_School_Systems_Final.pdf.

Becta. (2007). *Harnessing technology review 2007: Progress and impact of technology in education: Summary report.* Retrieved July 16, 2008, from http://publications.becta.org.uk/display.cfm?resID=33980.

Becta. (2008a). *Interactive whiteboards and enhancing teacher efficiency.* Available from http://schools.becta.org.uk/index.php?section=tl&cat code=ss_tl_use_02&rid=11910.

Becta. (2008b). *Harnessing technology review 2008.* Retrieved November 20, 2008, from http://publications.becta.org.uk/display.cfm?cfid=1098735&cftoken=c1b47a046bdd67e3-B79E87B1-C7E1-204D-79A221475A000DD2&page=1835.

Department for Education and Skills (DfES). (2005). *Harnessing technology: Transforming learning and children's services.* London. Available from http://www.dfes.gov.uk/publications/e-strategy/docs/e-strategy.pdf. Retrieved November 20, 2008.

ERNIST ICT school portraits. (2004). European Schoolnet. Retrieved November 18, 2008, from Schoolnet http://www.eun.org/insight-pdf/schoolportraits/ERNIST_ICT_schoolportaits.pdf.

Fullan, M. (2005). Professional learning communities writ large. In R. Dufour, & R. Eaker (Eds.), *On common ground: The power of professional learning communities.* Bloomington, IN: Solution Tree.

Fullan, M. (2007). Retrieved November 30, 2007, from http://www.michael fullan.ca/resource_assets/07_Keynote.pdf.

Futuresource Consulting. (2008). Interactive displays/ICT products market. *Quarterly Insight, State of the Market report,* Quarter 1, 2008. Unpublished presentation.

Glover, D., & Miller, D. (2001). *Missioners, Tentatives and Luddites: Leadership challenges for school and classroom posed by the introduction of interactive whiteboards into schools in the United Kingdom.* Part of the Symposium: New Technologies and Educational Leadership at the British Educational Management and Administration Society Conference, Newport Pagnell, UK. Retrieved November 18, 2008, from http://www.keele.ac.uk/depts/ed/iaw/Missioners.pdf.

Her Majesty's Inspectors of Education. (2005). *The integration of information and communications technology in Scottish schools*. Retrieved July 16, 2008, from http://www.hmie.gov.uk/documents/publication/EvICT%20Final%2018%20Oct.html.

Higgins, S., Falzon, C., Hall, I., Moseley, D., Smith, F., Smith, H., & Wall, K. (2005, April). Embedding ICT in the literacy and numeracy strategies. Newcastle: University of Newcastle on Tyne.

Higgins, S., & Moseley, D. (2002). Raising achievement in literacy through ICT. In M. Monteith, *Teaching primary literacy with ICT.* Buckingham: Open University Press.

IWBNet. (2008). *Richardson Primary 2003: Whole-school adoption of IWBs.* Retrieved July 16, 2008, from http://www.iwb.net.au/advice/case studies/richardson/1-intro.htm.

Kent, P. (2008). *Interactive whiteboards: A practical guide for primary teachers*. Melbourne: Macmillan Masterclass.

Kitchen, S., Finch, S., & Sinclair, R. (2007). *Harnessing technology schools survey 2007*. Coventry: Becta. Retrieved July 16, 2008, from http://partners. becta.org.uk/index.php?section=rh&catcode=_re_rp_02&rid=14110.

Lee, B., & Boyle, M. (2004). The teachers tell their story. *IWBNet*. Retrieved July 16, 2008 from http://www.iwb.net.au/advice/research/documents/ TeachersStory1.pdf.

Lee, M., & Boyle, M. (2003). *The educational effects and implications of the interactive whiteboard strategy of Richardson Primary School: A brief review*. Retrieved July 16, 2008, from http://www.richardsonps.act.edu. au/interactive_whiteboard_initiative.

Lee, M., & Boyle, M. (2004, March). Richardson Primary School: The Richardson Revolution. *Educare News*.

Lee, M., & Gaffney, M. (Eds.). (2008). *Leading a digital school.* Melbourne: ACER Press.

Lee, M., & Winzenried, A. (2006), Interactive whiteboards: Achieving total teacher usage. *Australian Educational Leader, 28*(3), 22–25.

Leithwood, K., & Riehl, C. (2004). What we know about successful leadership. *The Practising Administrator*, (4), 4–7.

Marzano, R.J. (2003). *What works in schools: Translating research into action*. ASCD Publications.

Miller, D., Glover, D., & Averis, D. (2004). *Matching technology and pedagogy in teaching mathematics.* University of Keele: Department of Education, Staffordshire, UK. Retrieved January 12, 2009, from http://www.keele.ac.uk/depts/ed/iaw/docs/BERA%20Paper%20Sep%202004.pdf.

Miller, D., Glover, D., & Averis, D. (2005). *Developing pedagogic skills for the use of the interactive whiteboard in mathematics.* University of Keele: Department of Education, Staffordshire, UK. Retrieved January 12, 2009, from http://www.keele.ac.uk/depts/ed/iaw/docs/BERA%20Paper%20Sep%202005.pdf.

Miller, D., Glover, D., Averis, D., & Door, V. (2006). *From technology to professional development: How can the use of interactive whiteboards in initial teacher education change the nature of learning in secondary mathematics and modern languages?* University of Keele: Department of Education, Staffordshire, UK. Retrieved November 15, 2008, from http://www.keele.ac.uk/depts/ed/iaw/#pubs.

Naisbitt, J. (1984). *Megatrends.* London: Futura.

Passey, D. (2002). *ICT and school management: A review of selected literature.* Lancaster University: Department of Educational Research. Retrieved July 16, 2008, from http://partners.becta.org.uk/page_documents/research/ict_sm.pdf.

Passey, D. (2005). *Aston Pride ICT Project phase 1: Evaluation report on the 'ICT in the home pilot' in Prince J/I School.* Birmingham: Birmingham City Council. Retrieved October 15, 2008, from http://www.bgfl.org/bgfl/custom/files_uploaded/uploaded_resources/12590/Evaluation.doc.

Passey, D., Rogers, C. G., Machell, J., & McHugh, G. (2004). *The motivational effect of ICT on pupils.* London: DfES. Retrieved October 15, 2008, from http://www.dfes.gov.uk/research/data/uploadfiles/RR523new.pdf.

Prensky, M. (2001, October). Digital natives, digital immigrants. *On the Horizon, 9*(5). NCB University Press. Retrieved November 30, 2007, from http://www.marcprensky.com/writing/Prensky%20-%20Digital%20Natives,%20Digital%20Immigrants%20-%20Part1.pdf.

Prensky, M. (2006). *Don't bother me Mum, I'm learning.* St Paul, Minnesota: Paragon House.

Promethean Planet. (2008). Available at http://www.prometheanplanet.com/.

Schuck, S. & Kearney, M. (2007). *Exploring pedagogy with interactive whiteboards: A case study of six schools.* Sydney: University of Technology. Retrieved November 19, 2008, from http://www.ed-dev.uts.edu.au/teachered/research/iwbproject/home.html.

SMART Learning Marketplace. (2008). Retrieved November 20, 2008, from https://learningmarketplace.smarttech.com/Default.aspx?WT.mc_id= SLM_prodED_visit.

Somekh, B., Haldene, M., Jones, K., Lewin, C., Steadman, S., Scrimshaw, P., Sing, S., Bird, K., Cummings, J., Downing, B., Harber Stuart, T., Jarvis, J., Mavers, D., & Woodrew, D. (2007), *Evaluation of the Primary Schools Whiteboard Expansion Project. Report to the Department for Education and Skills.* Manchester Metropolitan University: Centre for ICT, Pedagogy and Learning Education & Social Research Institute. Retrieved November 20, 2008, from http://partners.becta.org.uk/index. php?section=rh&catcode=_re_rp_02&rid=14422.

Underwood, J.D.M., Somekh, B., Cooke, A., Dillon, G., Lewin, C., Mavers, D., & Saxon, D. (2004). *Evaluation of the DfES ICT Test Bed Project: First annual report 2003.* Coventry, UK: Becta. Retrieved November 20, 2008, from http://www.evaluation.icttestbed.org.uk/about.

Venezky, R., & Davis, C. (2002, March). *Quo Vademus? The transformation of schooling in a networked world.* OECD/CERI.

Wikipedia: The free encyclopedia. (2008). Whiteboard. FL: Wikimedia Foundation, Inc. Last edited 18.33, June 25. Retrieved June 30, 2008, from http://en.wikipedia.org/wiki/Whiteboard.

You've read about it, now do something about it!

We hope this book has challenged you to think about the ways in which you approach teaching with an IWB. To build on these ideas, we're creating an online community of global IWB users... a place where you can be part of the ongoing conversation, learning and sharing with each other.

Come join the Revolution!
<www.iwbrevolution.com>

Chris <betchaboy@gmail.com>
and
Mal <mallee@mac.com>.

INDEX